THE PEOPLE OF BARBADOS

1625-1875

THE PEOPLE OF BARBADOS

1625-1875

By
David Dobson

CLEARFIELD

Published for Clearfield Company by
Genealogical Publishing Company

ISBN 9780806359076

INTRODUCTION

Barbados is the most easterly of the many islands of the Caribbean. Barbados was bypassed by the Spanish and Portuguese in the sixteenth century probably as it did not possess the gold and silver that they sought and discovered elsewhere in the Americas. As the indigenous inhabitants were long gone by the time the English found Barbados in 1625, it was available for settlement. Captain John Powell claimed Barbados for the Crown of England in 1625, and two years later the first shipload of settlers arrived from England.

The island was ideal for the production of tobacco, sugar, and cotton; consequently, soon entrepreneurs arrived from England aiming to produce such crops and market them in England and to some extent in Europe. These planters and merchants brought with them skilled artisans, many of whom arrived as indentured servants, and to a lesser extent rebels and criminals shipped in chains to be sold there. White Europeans were unwilling to perform hard labour in tropical plantations, and before long slaves were brought from Africa.

Most of the white population came from England and Wales, with a minority from Ireland and Scotland. [NB I have treated the Scots in my book 'Barbados and Scotland, Links 1627-1877, Baltimore, 2005]. There was also a considerable number of Sephardic Jews there, who had been encouraged by Oliver Cromwell to settle in Barbados to avoid persecution of the Spanish Inquisition. By the early eighteenth century, with the productive lands fully allocated and a growing population, a significant migration occurred from Barbados to the Leeward Islands, the Windward Islands, Jamaica, and as far north as South Carolina where the plantation economies were rapidly expanding. Planters, indentured servants, merchants, and African slaves thus became two stage migrants within the Americas. Slavery was abolished in Barbados in 1834, though the island remained a British colony until 1966 when it became fully independent.

This book is based on research into manuscript and published sources, mainly located in Great Britain but also in Barbados.

David Dobson, Dundee, Scotland, 2020

PEOPLE OF BARBADOS, 1625-1875

ABBADY, Reverend ISRAEL, born 1729, died 8 September 1797. [Bridgetown gravestone]

ABARBANEL, BENJAMIN, in Bridgetown, 1772. [BDA.Levy]

ABARBANEL, ISAAC, born 1709, died 30 November 1756. [Bridgetown gravestone

ABERDEIN, ROBERT, Customs Collector of Barbados letters, 1818 to 1836. [Sheffield Library; Wh.M.446i]

ABOAB, MOSES, in Bridgetown, 1772. [BDA.Levy]

ABOF, ISACK, with 2 children, in St Michael's, Barbados, in 1680. [HOT.449]

ABRAHAM, AGNES, from Barbados aboard the ketch Francis and Susan, master Phillip Knill, bound for Boston on 1 May 1679. [TNA]

ABUDIENT, ABRAHAM, from Barbados aboard the ketch Phoenix, master Robert Flexny, bound for Antigua on 25 November 1679. [TNA]; died 3 July 1697, Bridgetown gravestone]

ADAMS, GEORGE, from Barbados aboard the Adventure, master William Johnson, bound for London on 2 May 1679. [TNA]

ADAMS, GEORGE, Deputy Assistant General, married Miss Barclay, eldest daughter of George Barclay, in St Michael's Cathedral on 10 February 1825. [The Barbadian iii]

ADAMS, JOHN, a mariner aboard the Elizabeth in Carlisle Bay, Barbados, probate 1655 PCC

ADDAMS, MARY, wife of Samuel Adams, died 15 December 1672. [Christ Church MI]

ADAMS, THOMAS, from Barbados aboard the Defiance, master William Creed, bound for London on 26 April 1679. [TNA]

ADAMSON, GEORGE, from Barbados aboard the ketch Unity, master James Rainey, bound for Virginia on 26 April 1679. [TNA]

AGAZIS, Reverend, arrived in Bridgetown aboard the Mercy in February 1825. [The Barbadian iii]

AIR, SARAH, from Barbados aboard the sloop Katherine, master Andrew Gall, bound for Antigua on 25 November 1679. [TNA]

AKERS, WILLIAM, died in Barbados, Admin. 1660, PCC

ALBERT, ANN, from Barbados aboard the Mary, master Nicholas Lockwood, bound for Carolina on 28 April 1679. [TNA]

ALEXANDER, ANDREW, a merchant in St Michael's, Barbados, probate, 4 July 1744. [TNA.Prob.11.734.199]

ALLAMBY, WILLIAM, born around 1606, died 4 October 1678. [St Thomas gravestone]

ALLEN, Colonel John, of Backhall, Barbados, died in London on 29 October 1737. [GM.7.701]

ALLEN, MARGARET, daughter of John Foster Allen, married David Hall in Barbados on 21 May 1811. [GM.81.187]

ALLEN, PHILIP, born 1624, a merchant, died 12 November 1660, husband of Damaris ..., parents of Tamasin. [St Michael's MI]

ALLAN, ROBERT, a merchant in Belfast, trading with Barbados in 1726. [NRS.AC9.967]

ALLEYNE ANNIE, second daughter of Sir Reynold Alleyne of Alleynedale Hall, Barbados, married W. Fitzherbert, eldest son of Sir H. Fitzherbert, in Barbados on 20 February 1836. [GM.ns.5.544]

ALLEYNE, CHRISTIAN DOTTIN, fourth daughter of John Gay Alleyne in Barbados, married Reverend H. Withy, in Cheltenham on 26 April 1829. [GM.99.366]

ALLEYNE, DOUGLAS, Captain of the 37th Regiment, eldest son of Henry Alleyne in Barbados, married Ada Graves, only child of Charles Twistleton Graves, a former Captain of the Royal Irish Fusiliers, great grand-daughter of the 10th Lord Saye and Sele, in Kensington on 11 January 1865. [GM.ns.2/18.237]

ALLEYNE, ELIZABETH GIBBONS, wife of John Foster Alleyne, President of the Council of Barbados, died in Clifton, Gloucestershire, on 12 February 1820. [GM.90.282]

ALLEYNE, FITZHERBERT, second son of Sir Reynold A Alleyne, married Anna Maria Best, second daughter of Sir R Bowcher Clarke the Chief Justice of Barbados and St Lucia, in Barbados on 23 March 1854. [GM.ns.42.70]

ALLEYNE, GEORGE HENRY, born 9 August 1821, died 16 December 1884. [St Philip's MI]

ALLEYNE, J.G., arrived in Bridgetown aboard the Concord from Bristol in February 1825. [The Barbadian iii]

ALLEYNE, MARIA LOUISE, youngest daughter of H G Alleyne in Barbados, married John Fordyce of the Bengal Infantry, in Paris on 15 February 1842. [GM.ns.17.541]

ALLEYNE, MARY SPIRE, eldest daughter of Sir John Gay Alleyne in Barbados, died in Weston-super-Mare on 10 January 1862. [GM.ns.2/12.242]

ALLEYNE, PHILLIPA, daughter of Sir R A Alleyne, married Hampden Clement in Barbados in July 1831. [GM.101.268]

ALLEYN, REIGNOLD, a gentleman in St David's, Barbados in 1651. [CLRO.Deposition.9]

ALLEYNE, REYNOLD, of Mount Alleyne in the parish of St James, born1700, died 30 June 1749. [Christ Church MI]

ALLEYNE, Sir REYNOLD ABEL, born 10 June 1789, died 14 February 1870, husband of Rebecca......, born 23 August 1794, died 5 June 1860. [St Lucy's MI]

ALLEYNE, SAMUEL MAYNARD, of Ridgway Estate, born 25 August 1809, drowned at Bathsheba on 20 May 1847. [St Thomas MI]

ALLEYNE, THOMAS, died in Barbados on 13 May 1775. [GM.45.255]

3

ALLEYNE, ..., son of J G Newton Alleyne, was born at Turner's Hall, Barbados, on 16 May 1852. [GM.ns.38.193]

ALLIN, ELIAZER, from Barbados aboard the <u>Prudence and Mary,</u> master Jacob Green bound for Boston on 27 May 1679. [TNA]

ALLISON, THOMAS, from Barbados aboard the <u>John's Adventure</u>, master Edward Winslow, bound for Jamaica on 14 June 1679. [TNA]

ALSOP, KATHERINE, from Barbados aboard the sloop <u>Katherine</u>, master Andrew Gall, bound for Antigua on 25 November 1679. [TNA]

AMBLER, JOHN, the representative for James Town, Barbados, died in 1766, [GM.36.405]

AMES, CHARLES, born 1778, son of ...... Ames in Colchester, Essex, died in Bridgetown, Barbados, on 1 July 1806. [GM.76.874]

AMEY, WILLIAM, of the Commissariat, died in July 1824. [The Barbadian ii]

AMWYL, Lieutenant Colonel, of the 4th Regiment, married Senhouse Barrow, daughter of J. Barrow, in Barbados on 22 October 1822. [GM.92.560]

ANDERSON, MARGARET, from Barbados aboard the ketch <u>Unity,</u> master James Ramsay, bound for Virginia on 28 April 1679. [TNA]

ANDERSON, WILLIAM, in Barbados, eldest son of John Anderson a merchant in Leith, a deed, 9 June 1819. [NRS.RD5.166.130]

ANDRADA, DANIEL DA COSTA, died 1802. [Bridgetown gravestone]

ANDREWE, JOHN, in Barbados, probate, 1654, PCC

ANGELO, MICHAEL, of the War Office, married Ann Bell Grant, fourth daughter of William Grant, a barrister in Barbados, in Paddington on 24 April 1862. [GM.ns.2/12.775]

ANGLIM, THOMAS R., married Miss White, daughter of T. W. White, on 13 December 1824. [The Barbadian ii]

ANTHONY, JOHN, a yeoman, an indentured servant bound via Bristol to Barbados in December 1660. [BRO]

ANTUNES, GABRIELL, with two children, in St Michael's, Barbados, in 1680. [HOT.450]

APPLEWHAITE, THOMAS, born 1690, a Member of HM Council of Barbados, died 14 June 1749, husband of Elizabeth Applewhaite, born 1691, died 11 April 1750. [St George's MI]

ARCHER, JOHN, born 1811, died 19 January 1860, husband of Mary Edward, parents of Sarah Elliott Archer, born 1834, died 1 April 1858. [St Lucy's gravestone]

ARCHER, JOHN VASSALL, only son of John Giddies Archer in Barbados, died in Clifton on 26 October 1806. [GM.76.1169]

ARCHER, Mrs, born 1777, daughter of John Vassall in Bath, wife of John Gittons Archer in Barbados, died in Clifton on 27 December 1806. [GM.76.1254]

ARIS, JOHN, from Barbados aboard the Endeavour, master James Gilbert, bound for London on 20 March 1679. [TNA]

ARIST, HENRY, from Barbados aboard the Industry, master James Porter, bound for Bristol on 22 May 1679. [TNA]

ARMITAGE, HENRY, from Barbados aboard the Society, master William Guard, bound for Boston on 11 March 1679. [TNA]

ARMSTRONG, ANN, aboard the Francis, master Peter Jeffreys, bound for Antigua on 29 April 1679. [TNA]

ARON, ABRAHAM BURGES, with two children, in St Michael's, Barbados, in 1680. [HOT.449]

ARROBAS, MOSES, with four children, in St Michael's, Barbados, in 1680. [HOT.449]

ASHBY, ..., son of Nathan Ashby, was born in October 1825. [The Barbadian iii]

ARTHUR, KATHERINE, from Barbados aboard the ketch Prosperous, master David Hogg, bound for Virginia on 2 May 1679. [TNA]

ASFORDBY, EDWARD, a bachelor, died in Barbados, Admin., 1654, PCC

ASTONS, ROBERT, an indentured servant bound via Bristol to Barbados in December 1660. [BRO]

ATHERTON, WILLIAM, from Barbados aboard the Nathaniel, master William Clarke, bound for Boston on 8 October 1679. [TNA]

ATKINS, Sir JONATHAN, Governor around 1680.

ATKINS, SARAH, with 1 child, in St Michael's, Barbados, in 1680. [HOT.450]

ATKINSON, CHRISTOPHER, married Elizabeth, daughter of William Duke in November 1825. [The Barbadian iii]

ATKINSON, HUMPHREY, died in Barbados, Admin. 1649, PCC

ATKINSON, ROBERT, a widower who died in Barbados, Admin., 1658, PCC

ATKINSON, THOMAS, jr., an author from Glasgow, died on passage to Barbados on 10 October 1833. [GM.104.670]

ATKINSON, TIMOTHY, a mariner in Barbados, probate, 3 July 1746, [TNA.Prob.11.748.88]

AUSTIN, ELIZA HOWARD, died in Bridgetown, Barbados, on 16 November 1848. [GM.ns.31.222]

AUSTIN, JOHN, a surgeon, from Barbados, married Letitia Cartwright, in Notting Hill on 17 April 1801. [GM.71.371]; she died on 19 November 1801, having arrived in Barbados in September 1801. [St Michael's MI]

AUSTIN, MARY EWING, daughter of the late John Austin in Barbados, married Reverend James Lugar BA of Sussex College, Cambridge, and of Three Friends Plantation in Essequibo, at Trinity Church, Essequibo, on 18 August 1825. [The Barbadian iii]

AUSTIN, Reverend WILTSHIRE S., married D. Webster, daughter of Dr
Webster, at St George's Church in April 1824. [The Barbadian.ii]

AUSTIN, Miss, daughter of Reverend Hugh William Austin in
Barbados, married Captain Goldfinch of the Oxford Militia, in Bath on
17 January 1807. [GM.77.88]

AUTON, Lieutenant Colonel, born 1779, died at Bell Vue, Barbados,
on 9 September 1856. [GM.ns.2/1.657]

AVERY, MARY, from Barbados aboard the Golden Fleece, master Henry
Pascall, bound for London on 18 August 1679. [TNA]

BABB, MARGERY, born 1742, died 26 January 1811, wife of Benjamin
Babb. [St Lucy's gravestone]

BACH, GUY, a merchant in Barbados in 1644. [CLRO.Deposition.2]

BADDINGTON, THOMAS, 'a servant belonging to Thomas Gladdin',
from Barbados aboard the barque Adventure, master Edward
Duffield, bound for Jamaica on 7 November 1679. [TNA]

BAGNALL, JOHN, from Barbados aboard the sloop Rutter, master
Edward Duffield, bound for Jamaica on 4 April 1679. [TNA]

BAGWELL, FRANCIS, from Barbados aboard the ketch Calieta, master
Samuel Paul, bound for Topsham on 29 April 1679. [TNA]

BAKER, DANIEL, born 1615, bound from London aboard the Hopewell
to Barbados in February 1635. [TNA.E157.20]

BAKER, JOHN, a labourer from Barbados aboard the Friendship, master
John Williams, bound for London on 9 August 1679. [TNA]

BALFOUR, JAMES, from Barbados aboard the sloop True Friendship,
master Charles Callahan, bound for Antigua on 4 October 1679. [TNA]

BALL, JAMES, from Barbados aboard the Pelican, master John Cocke,
bound for London on 13 April 1679. [TNA]

BALRICK, THOMAS, from Barbados aboard the Hope, master Joseph Ball,
bound for London on 22 April 1679. [TNA]

BALSTON, WILLIAM, died 26 October 1659. [Christ Church MI]

BANAM, JOHN, a houseboy in Bridewell, bound for Barbados in 1632. [Minutes of the Court of Bridewell]

BANCKS, JOSEPH, from Barbados, aboard the ketch William and Susan, master Ralph Parker, bound for New England on 22 March 1679. [TNA]

BANDINE, JOHN, a pensioner in the Barbados Hospital, probate, 8 June 1773, [TNA.Prob.11.988.287]

BANNISTER, RICHARD, from Barbados aboard the sloop True Friendship, master Charles Callahan, bound for Antigua on 4 October 1679. [TNA]

BANTON, JANE, a spinster, a yeoman, an indentured servant bound via Bristol to Barbados in December 1660. [BRO]

BANYSTER, JOHN, a grocer in London, with property in Barbados, probate 1654, PCC

BARBAULD, Mrs, born around 1742, sister of the late Dr Aikin, died in April 1825. 'she had a literary career'. [The Barbadian iii]

BARCLAY, MARGARET, second daughter of George Barclay in Barbados, married Charles Taddy, second son of Reverend John Taddy, in Bedfordshire on 8 Ma 1843. [GM.ns.20.87]

BARKER, JOHN, who died in Barbados, Admin., 1654, PCC

BARKER, Reverend, and his wife, arrived in Bridgetown aboard the Renewal in February 1825, from London. [The Barbadian iii]

BARKER, Reverend J C, in St George's, the Chaplain to the Bishop of Barbados, died on Tortula in 1842. [GM.ns.18.101]

BARNARD, HUMPHREY, sr., from Barbados, aboard the ketch, master George Conway, bound for Carolina on 27 March 1679. [TNA]

BARNARD, HUMPHREY, jr., from Barbados, aboard the ketch, master George Conway, bound for Carolina on 27 March 1679. [TNA]

BARNEWELL, ROBERT, from Barbados aboard the <u>Recovery,</u> master James Brown, bound for Jamaica on 29 December 1679. [TNA]

BARNES, NICHOLAS, from Barbados aboard the barque <u>Blessing,</u> master Francis Watlington, bound for Providence on 27 April 1679. [TNA]

BARRETT, SUSAN, daughter of Richard and Martha Barrett, died 9 April 1665. [St Michael's MI]

BARROW, ELIZA, daughter of J H Barrow, married William Grassett, in Barbados on 26 March 1818, [GM.88.368]

BARROW, JEREMIAH, in Bridgetown, 1772. [BDA.Levy]

BARROW, JOSEPH, in Bridgetown, 1772. [BDA.Levy]

BARROW, MARY KATHERINE, born 1833, wife of Joseph H Barrow, died 25 September 1859. [St Michael's MI]

BARROW, REBECCA, from Barbados aboard the <u>Ann and Jane,</u> master Richard Radford, bound for London on 18 December 1679. [TNA]

BARROW, SARAH, born 1741, wife of Haim Barrow, died 12 September 1823. [Bridgetown gravestone]

BARROW, SARAH, born 1742, wife of Joseph Barrow, died 10 March 1814. [Bridgetown gravestone]

BARROW, SENHOUSE, daughter of J Barrow in Barbados, married Lieutenant Colonel Amwyl of the 4th Regiment, in Barbados on 22 October 1822. [GM.92.560]

BARROW, SIMON, in Bridgetown, 1772. [BDA.Levy]

BARRUCH, ABRAHAM, with three children, in St Michael's, Barbados, in 1680. [HOT.449]

BARRUCH, ARON, with five children, in St Michael's, Barbados, in 1680. [HOT.449]

BARRUCH, REBECAH, with one child, in St Michael's, Barbados, in 1680. [HOT.450]

BARTON, CHRISTOPHER, from Barbados aboard the Barbados Merchant, master James Cock, bound for Virginia on 3 October 1679. [TNA]

BARTON, JAMES, from Barbados, aboard the ketch William and Susan, master Ralph Parker, bound for New England on 12 March 1679. [TNA]

BARWICK, SAMUEL, born 1669, died 1 January 1732, father of William, and Samuel, born 1702, died 4 June 1741. [St James, Hole Town, MI]

BARWILL, JOHN, from Barbados aboard the frigate Constant Warwick, Captain Ralph Delavall, bound for London on 1 March 1679. [TNA]

BASCOM, GRIFFIN, born 1790, from Demerara, died 9 June 1852. [St Thomas gravestone]

BASCOM, Mrs MARY, born 1747, wife of James Bascom, died 30 October 1789. [St Thomas gravestone]

BASCOM, WILHELMINA, born 1817, died 25 August 1892. [St Michael's gravestone]

BATE, MARGARET, a widow in Barbados, probate, 27 February 1720, PCC. [TNA.Prob.11.572.516]

BATES, RICHARD, from Barbados, aboard the Expedition, master John Harding, bound for London on 1 April 1679. [TNA]

BATSON, HENRY, a merchant in Barbados in 1650. [CLRO.Deposition.10]

BATSON, THOMAS, a merchant in Barbados, an attorney there in 1652. [CLRO.Dep.10]

BATTISON, JULIAN, from Barbados aboard the sloop Endeavour, master Thomas Shaw, bound for Carolina on 13 October 1679. [TNA]

BATTYN, Dr JOHN, died 7 January 1692, father of Elizabeth Battyn, born 1689, died 26 October 1736, wife of Edward Brace, and his grandson William Rees Battyn, born 1704, died 14 August 1734. [St George's MI]

BAYLEY, Sir FRANCIS SOUPER, born in Barbados, proprietor of Malvern St Joseph, Recorder of Prince of Wales Island, died there on 29 October 1824. [The Barbadian iii]

BEAKE, Major JAMES, in Barbados, an attorney for William Hudson a draper in London, a deposition, 1660. [CLRO.Deposition.10]

BEAMAN, RICHARD, died in Barbados, admin., 1658, PCC

BEARD, JOHN, from Barbados aboard the Friendship, master John Williams, bound for London on 9 August 1679. [TNA]

BEAVER, Reverend, and his wife, arrived in Bridgetown aboard the Renewal in February 1825, from London. [The Barbadian iii]

BECCLES, ELIZABETH CHRISTIAN, daughter of John Beccles the former Attorney General of Barbados, widow of Robert Augustus Hyndman in Demerara, died on 9 September 1834. [GM.104.554]

BECKLES, FORTESCUE H., died in June 1824. [The Barbadian.ii]

BECKELS, HENRY, of Barbados, married Miss Maxwell, on 28 September 1742. [GM.32.503]

BECKLES, H., son of the President of Barbados, married Susannah Henry, daughter of William Henry of Barbados, in Marylebone on 17 July 1838. [GM.ns.10.439]

BECKLES, JOHN, the Attorney General Barbados, letters, 1801. [NRS.GD46.17.20]

BECKLES, JOHN ALLEYNE, former President of Barbados, died on 14 July 1840. [GM.ns.14.446]; born 1778, former President of Barbados, Judge of the Vice Admiralty Court, Provincial Grand Master of Masons, died 14 July 1840. [St Michael's MI]

BECKLES, R., of the 3rd West Indian Regiment, only son of Robert Beckles in Barbados, grandson of John Alleyne Beckles a former President of Barbados, married Helen Rogers, youngest daughter of

John Rogers, in Westbury on Tyne, on 20 January 1852. [GM.ns.37.401]

BEDFORD, JOHN, born 1779, the Vice Admiralty Judge, died in Barbados on 30 September 1807. [GM.77.1172]; his widow died on passage from Barbados on 23 March 1808. [GM.78.459]

BEDFORD, PAUL, a gentleman of Barbados, from Portsmouth aboard the Favourite Betsey, bound for Barbados in April 1774. [TNA.T47.9/11]

BELGRAVE, CHARLOTTE, petitioned the Governor of Barbados on behalf of her husband imprisoned for debt, in 1804. [NRS.GD46.17.5]

BEMISTER, THOMAS, a bachelor from Southampton, died in Barbados, Admin., 1654, PCC

BENNET, JAMES, of Barbados, died in Thame on 6 February 1758. [GM.28.94]

BENNET, MARK, a merchant in Barbados, probate, 3 December 1646, PCC. [TNA.Prob.11.198.360]

BENNEY, EDWARD, born in Shrewsbury, Shropshire, on 24 June 1619, settled in St Joseph's, Barbados, in 1647, an Assemblyman and Representative, died 16 September 1701. [St Joseph's MI]

BENNY, JAMES, from Demerara, died in Barbados on 15 December 1820. [GM.91.186]

BENTLY, MARTIN, from Barbados aboard the ketch Mary and Sarah, master George Conway, bound for Providence, on 20 November 1679. [TNA]

BENSON, MARY, from Barbados aboard the sloop Endeavour, master Thomas Shaw, bound for Carolina on 9 October 1679. [TNA]

BENTALL, Mrs HENRY, born 1775, died in Bridgetown, Barbados, at the residence of her son Alexander Stewart, on 25 June 1845. [GM.ns.24.326]

BERESFORD, ELIZABETH KETURAH, born 1785, second daughter of Berwick Bruce MD in Barbados, widow of James Beresford of the Royal York Rangers 1st West India Regiment, died at the home of her son Berwick Beresford MD on 3 March 1852. [GM.ns.37.530]

BERKELEY, ANNE, eldest daughter of Lieutenant General S H Berkeley, Commanding Officer of the West Indies, great-grand-daughter of Dr Alexander Bruce in Barbados, married Captain A Carden of the 60th Rifles, in Barbados on 4 August 1847. [GM.ns.28.533]

BERNARD, DAVID, a planter in Barbados, died in 1773. [GM.43.581]

BERNEY, MARY, born 1708, died 17 July 1783, relict of Robert Berney. [St George's MI]

BERROW, CHRISTOPHER, from Barbados aboard the Society, master Edmund Ditty, bound for Bristol on 25 May 1679. [TNA]

BEST, FRANCES MARIA, second daughter of John Rycroft Best in Barbados, married S R Wybault, in Charlton Kings, on 2 June 1846. [GM.ns.26.197]

BEST, JOHN, was appointed a Councillor of Barbados in 1774. [PC.Col.V.563]

BEVELL, JOHN, born 1729, a merchant in Barbados, from London aboard the Richmond, bound for Barbados in January 1774. [TNA.T47.9/11]

BEVEMSTER, ELIAH, from Barbados aboard the Friendship, master John Williams, bound for London on 11 August 1679. [TNA]

BICKLE, THOMAS, from Barbados aboard the sloop Mayflower, master Edward Hubbert, bound for Bermuda on 7 April 1679. [TNA]

BILENFANTE, DEBORAH, married Simon Meffiat in Barbados in 1768. [GM.38.19.8]

BILFORD, JAMES, from Barbados aboard the pink Sea Venture, master George Battersby, bound for Antigua on 5 March 1679. [TNA]

BINCKS, CHARLES, from Barbados aboard the Experiment, master Allan Cock bound for London on 5 May 1679. [TNA]

BIRD, HENRY, from Barbados aboard the Amity, master Benjamin Grove, bound for London on 1 July 1679. [TNA]

BISHOP, ANNE, a spinster, an indentured servant bound via Bristol to Barbados in December 1660. [BRO]

BISHOP, ELIZABETH MACLEAN, born 1804, eldest daughter of Charles Kyd Bishop in Barbados, wife of Henry Prater, died in London on 31 August 1846. [GM.ns.26.441]

BISHOP, ROBERT, from Barbados aboard the Experiment, master Allan Cock, bound for London on 10 May 1679. [TNA]

BISHOP, ROBERT, born 1680, died 16 September 1715, husband of Mary Forbes, born 1686, died 26 May 1734. Parents of Mary Morris Bishop, born 1710, died 25 May 1743. [St Philip's gravestone]

BISHOP, THOMAS, from Barbados aboard the Virgin, master Thomas Alamby, bound for the Leeward Islands on 4 October 1679. [TNA]

BISHOP, WILLIAM, was appointed a Councillor of Barbados in 1773. [PC.Col.V.562]; President of the Council of Barbados, letters, 1800-1801. [NRS.GD46.7.1]

BISPHAM, JOHN R., of Barbados, married Catharine Gordon, daughter of Daniel Gordon at St Lucia on 21 September 1825. [The Barbadian iii]

BISPHAM, THOMAS M., eldest son of Gedney C. Bispham MD, married Elizabeth Clarke, daughter of Thomas Clarke, on 1 January 1824. [The Barbadian.ii]; their daughter was born at Clyde Bank on 2 January 1825. [The Barbadian iii]

BISPHAM, Mrs, widow of Gedney Clark Bispham MD, died in March 1824. [The Barbadian.ii]

BLACKBURN, THOMAS C., married Mary Delph, both of Bridgetown, on 21 September 1824. [The Barbadian ii]

BLACKLEECH, JOHN, sr., from Barbados aboard the ketch Mayflower, master Robert Kitchin, bound for Boston on 8 May 1679. [TNA]

BLACKLEECH, JOHN, jr., from Barbados aboard the ketch Mayflower, master Robert Kitchin, bound for Boston on 8 May 1679. [TNA]

BLADES, ANTHONY, born 1611, bound from London aboard the Hopewell to Barbados in February 1635. [TNA.E157.20]

BLAKE, JOHN, from Barbados aboard the sloop Resolution, master John Ingleby, bound for Montserrat on 18 February 1679. [TNA]

BLAKE, P., from Sevenoaks in Kent, married John Sober in Barbados on 6 November 1760. [GM.18.102]

BLAND, ELIZA, who died in Barbados, Admin., 1657, PCC

BLARE, EDWARD, a gentleman in Barbados, probate, 29 November 1717, PCC. [TNA.Prob.11.560.385]

BLENMAN, JONATHAN, Solicitor General of Barbados, died on 13 February 1807. [GM.77.484]

BLENMAN, JONATHAN, born 1785, son of John Blenman, the Solicitor General of Barbados, died in Penzance on 22 July 1843. [GM.ns.20.329]

BLENMAN, Mrs, widow of Reverend Timothy Blenman, late in Barbados, died in Clifton, Bristol, on 27 November 1820. [GM.20.571]

BLUNT, GEORGE, from Barbados aboard the Lisbon Merchant, master Roger Whitfield, bound for New York on 2 October 1679. [TNA]

BOBYER, SAMUEL, from Bristol, died in Barbados, Admin. 1660, PCC

BODINGHAM, JOHN, from Barbados aboard the Friendship, master John Williams, bound for New England on 14 August 1679. [TNA]

BODKIN, NICHOLAS, from Barbados aboard the Young William, master Thomas Cornish, bound for Virginia on 1 August 1679. [TNA]

BOLTON, AMBROSE, from Barbados aboard the New Concord, master James Strutt, bound for London on 17 May 1679. [TNA]

BOLTON, SAMUEL, from Barbados aboard the Bare, master William Dickens, bound for London on 7 July 1679. [TNA]

BOND, FRANCIS, born in Bodmyn, Cornwall, in November 1636, died 3 August 1699. [St Michael's MI]

BOND, THOMAS, from Barbados aboard the ketch Elizabeth, master John Fletcher, bound for Boston on 29 May 1679. [TNA]

BONHAM, Lieutenant Colonel, of the 69th Regiment, married Agnes Skeete, niece of William Bishop the Governor of Barbados, in Bridgetown, Barbados, on 26 February 1800. [GM.70.588]

BOVELL, ..., daughter of John Bovell, was born on 6 November 1824. [The Barbadian ii]; Frances, infant daughter of John Bovell of The Hermitage, died in January 1825. [The Barbadian iii]

BOVELL, MARY, only daughter of J. Bovell MD in Barbados, married Reverend M Payne Hope in Christon Somerset on 16 July 1834. [GM.104.312]

BOWCHER, Reverend ROBERT, born 1732, Rector of Christ Church parish for 22 years, died 25 November 1795. [Christ Church MI]

BOWDEN, JAMES, a merchant from London, died 4 March 1821. [St Michael's MI]

BOWDLER, ANDREW, from Barbados aboard the James, master William Sweetland, bound for New York on 13 February 1679. [TNA]

BOWEN, F. JACKMAN, born 1846, died 1 July 1865. [St Michael's MI]

BOWHANE, TEAG, from Barbados aboard the Society, master Edmund Ditty, bound for Boston on 2 June 1679. [TNA]

BOWYER, GEORGE, a vagrant in Bridewell, bound for Barbados in 1632. [Bridewell Court Minutes]

BOX, ANN, from Barbados aboard the ketch Prosperous, master David Fogg, bound for Virginia on 6 May 1679. [TNA]

BOXILL, WILLIAM MD, born 1777, from Barbados, died in London on 16 October 1846. [GM.ns.26.663]

BOYCE, JONATHAN, died on Baker's Estate, St Peter, on 27 October 1824. [The Barbadian ii]

BOYLE, ..., son of Captain Cavendish Boyle, was born in Barbados on 11 August 1847. [GM.ns.28.422]; another son was born there on 29 May 1849. [GM.ns.32.197]

BOYLSTON, THOMAS, who died in Barbados, Admin., 1657, PCC

BOYNA, DANIEL, with three children, in St Michael's, Barbados, in 1680. [HOT.449]

BRACE, EDWARD, in St Michael, Barbados, probate, 17 March 1744. [TNA.Prob.11.732.239]

BRADBOURNE, EDWARD, a merchant in Barbados, 1660. [CLRO.deposition.10]

BRADFORD, JOHN, in Barbados, Admin., 1650, PCC

BRADLEY, MICHAEL, from Barbados aboard the Amity, master Benjamin Grove, bound for London on 2 July 1679. [TNA]

BRAITHWAITE, ELIZA GITTENS, born 1783, wife of John Braithwaite, died on 15 November 1805. [St Philip's MI]

BRAITHWAITE, ELIZABETH JANE, eldest daughter of Miles Braithwaite in Barbados, married Ledeatt Redwood, eldest son of George Washington Ledeatt of Antigua, in London on 13 January 1846. [GM.ns.25.308]

BRAITHWAITE, JOHN, born in Barbados on 25 October 1722, died in Epsom, Surrey, on 21 September 1800. [St Michael's MI]

BRAITHWAITE, JOHN, Agent of Barbados, letters, 1800. [NRS.GD46.17.14]

BRAITHWAITE, MILES, third son of M. Braithwaite in Barbados, died at Fort Twiss, Hythe, Kent, on 26 March 1837. [GM.ns.2/2.627]

BRAITHWAITE, ..., daughter of Miles Braithwaite jr., was born at Palmer's, St Philip, in November 1824. [The Barbadian ii]

BRAITHWAITE, Reverend Robert, born 1723, Anglican minister of St Philip's from 1753 to 1792, died in 1811; was appointed a Councillor of Barbados in 1768. [PC.Col.V.562]

BRANBY, ELIZA, 'a servant belonging to David Watkins', from Barbados aboard the sloop Rutter, master Edward Duffield, bound for Jamaica on 30 September 1679. [TNA]

BRANDON, ABRAHAM, in Bridgetown, 1772. [BDA.Levy]

BRANDON, DAVID, born 1734, died 6 October 1796. [Bridgetown gravestone]; in Bridgetown, 1772. [BDA.Levy]

BRAUGH, C., born 1772, a merchant formerly in Barbados, died in Bristol on 9 February 1812. [GM.82.391]

BREAD, ARTHUR, from Barbados aboard the ketch Phoenix, master Robert Flexny, bound for the Leeward Islands on 25 November 1679. [TNA]

BREAD, THOMAS, from Barbados aboard the Providence, master Timothy Pront, bound for Boston on 22 June 1679. [TNA]

BREAD, THOMAS, from Barbados aboard the ketch Phoenix, master Robert Flexny, bound for the Leeward Islands on 25 November 1679. [TNA]

BREARLY, MARTIN, from Barbados aboard the White Fox, master John Lee, bound for London on 5 May 1679. [TNA]

BREDIN, ..., daughter of Major Edgar Grantham Bredin of the Royal Artillery, was born in Gunhill, Barbados, on 8 September 1865. [GM.ns.3/1.220]

BRENAN, THOMAS, from Barbados, died in Westerham, Kent, on 17 February 1814. [GM.84.410]

BRETT, JOHN, from Barbados aboard the Honor, master Thomas Warren, bound for London on 15 April 1679. [TNA]

BRIGHT, ROBERT, of Barbados, a will, 1758. [BRO.ms8015]

BROCKDON, HUMPHREY, a merchant, 1673. [St Michael's MI]

BROGRAVE, HENRY, from Barbados, aboard the Malaga Merchant, master Roger Homer, bound for London on 21 July 1679. [TNA]

BROOK, THOMAS, from Barbados aboard the Recovery, master James Brown, bound for Jamaica on 24 December 1679. [TNA]

BROOMFIELD, GEORGE, married Elizabeth Millman, in August 1825. [The Barbadian iii]

BROUGH, HANNAH, born 1777, wife of Charles Brough, died 31 January 1807. [St Michael's MI]

BROWN, FRANCIS, from Barbados aboard the barque Blessing, master Francis Watling, bound for Bermuda on 16 September 1679. [TNA]

BROWN, Mrs HAWKINS, born 1753, daughter of Edward Hay the Governor of Barbados, and wife of Isaac H. Brown, MP, died on 11 April 1802. [GM.72.473]

BROWN, HUGH, from Barbados aboard the Bachelor, master William Knott, bound for London on 12 July 1679. [TNA]

BROWN, JAMES THOMAS, born 1830, died 21 October 1852. [St Philip's MI]

BROWNE, JOB, a merchant from London, settled in Barbados by December 1659. [CLRO.Deposition.9]

BROWN, JOHN, from Barbados aboard the ketch Providence, master Mark Hunking, bound for Boston on 16 May 1679. [TNA]

BROWN, JOHN, a stationer from Lincolnshire, an indentured servant bound via Liverpool for Barbados in 1698. [LRO]

BROWN, JOHN, was appointed a Councillor of Barbados in 1768. [PC.Col.V.562]

BROWNE, PHILLIP, a yeoman, a yeoman, an indentured servant bound via Bristol to Barbados in December 1660. [BRO]

BROWN, RACHEL, from Barbados aboard the barque Adventure, master Christopher Borrow, bound for Antigua on 17 February 1679. [TNA]

BROWNE, THOMAS, a bachelor in Barbados, Admin., 1649, PCC

BROWN, WILLIAM, from Barbados aboard the Merchants' Adventure, master George Greigs, bound for Liverpool on 7 May 1679. [TNA]

BROWN, Reverend WILLIAM, MA of Jesus College, Cambridge, arrived in Barbados from York Upper Canada, on 19 April 1825. [The Barbadian iii]

BROWNING, ANN, from Barbados aboard the Martin, master Christopher Martin, bound for Newfoundland on 1 April 1679. [TNA]

BRUCE, JAMES, in Barbados, died 19 September 1749. [GM.19.429]

BUCHANAN, GEORGINA BRUCE, only daughter of Captain Buchanan of the 62nd Regiment, great grand-daughter of James Bruce the Chief Judge of Barbados, married William Downes Jewill, in Barbados on 26 November 1844. [GM.ns.23.420]

BULKLY, WILLIAM, from Barbados aboard the <u>Ann and Jane,</u> master Richard Radford, bound for London on 24 December 1679. [TNA]

BUTLER, JOHN, from Barbados aboard the ketch <u>New London,</u> master Adam Pickett, bound for London on 4 July 1679. [TNA]

BURCH, WILLIAM, died in Barbados, Admin., 1654, PCC

BURCHALL, C., arrived in Bridgetown aboard the <u>Concord</u> from Bristol in February 1825. [The Barbadian iii]

BURGOS, ABRAHAM, from Barbados aboard the ketch <u>William and John,</u> master John Sanders, bound for New England on 11 April 1679. [TNA]

BURGOS, ELIAS, in Bridgetown, 1772. [BDA.Levy]

BURGES, RACHEL, with six children, in St Michael's, Barbados, in 1680. [HOT.450]

BURGOS, RACHEL. in Bridgetown, 1772. [BDA.Levy]

BURKE, JEFFREY, from Barbados aboard the sloop <u>True Friendship,</u> master Charles Callahan, bound for Antigua on 30 December 1679. [TNA]

BURNE, DENNIS, a servant belonging to Mr Henry Applewhite, from Barbados aboard the ketch <u>Prosperous,</u> master David Fogg, bound for Virginia on 6 May 1679. [TNA]

BURNELL, JOHN, formerly a grocer in Bristol, settled in Barbados by 1649. [CLRO.Deposition.3]

BURROWES, JOHN, died at Fontabelle on 25 November 1824. [The Barbadian ii]

BURROWS, THOMAS F., born in Barbados, died in Demerara on 6 April 1825. [The Barbadian iii]

BUSHELL, THOMAS, a bachelor, died in Barbados, Admin. 1659 PCC

BUSHELL, WILLIAM, from Barbados aboard the Pearl, master Richard Williams, bound for Antigua on 17 April 1679. [TNA]

BUTCHER, JAMES, born 1776, a physician and surgeon, died 9 March 1856. [St Michael's MI]

BUTCHER, JOHN, from Barbados aboard the sloop True Friendship, master Charles Callahan, bound for Antigua on 4 October 1679. [TNA]

BUTLER, ELINOR, 'a servant belonging to William Bulkley', from Barbados aboard the ketch Neptune, master John Knott, bound for Virginia on 19 August 1679. [TNA]

BUTLER, JOHN, died on 7 November 1825. [The Barbadian iiiBUTLER, WALTER, from Barbados aboard the ketch John and Sarah, master James Shoare, bound for New York on 20 October 1679. [TNA]

BUZAGLO, ABRAHAM, in Bridgetown, 1772. [BDA.Levy]

BYAR, WOODRUFFE SINCLAIR, born 1810, died at Clifton near Bristol on 10 January 1852, husband of Henrietta Sharp, born 1824, died in Barbados on 15 March 1852. [St Philip's MI]

BYG, ROBERT, Governor of Barbados, died on 6 October1740. [GM.11.50]

BYNOE, BENJAMIN, principal clerk in the Protonotory's office, died in Bridgetown on 11 March 1824. [The Barbadian.ii]

CADELL, JOHN, a gentleman in Bristol, an indentured servant bound from Bristol to Barbados in April 1658. [BRO]

CADOGAN, ELIZABETH, born 1752, died 5 July 1842, her sister Dorothy Cadogan, born 1766, died 24 October 1851. [St Peter's, Speight Town, gravestone]

CALLEY, THOMAS, from Barbados in the ketch Neptune, master Joseph Knott, bound for Carolina on 13 August 1679. [TNA]

CALLENDER, Miss ELIZABETH, of Bridgetown, died in May 1824. [The Barbadian. ii]

CALLENDER, JOHN SPENCER, died in March 1825. [The Barbadian iii]

CALLENDER, MARY JANE, eldest daughter of Nicholas Rice Callender of Barbados, married Henry Edward Sharpe a barrister at law and Solicitor General of Grenada, in April 1825. [The Barbadian iii]

CALENDAR, TIMOTHY, was appointed a Councillor of Barbados in 1782. [PC.Col.V.563]

CAMERON, ..., son of Eugene Hay Cameron a Lieutenant of the Royal Artillery, was born in Barbados on 23 May 1863. [GM.ns.2/15.94]

CAMPANELL, MORDECAI, from Barbados aboard the ketch Swallow, master Joseph Hardy, for New England on 1 April 1679. [TNA]

CANTING, DENNIS, from Barbados aboard the pink Mary, master Nicholas Lockwood, bound for Carolina on 10 March 1679. [TNA]

CAREW, THOMAS, from Barbados aboard the Benjamin of Topsham, master Robert Lyde, on 22 April 1679. [TNA]

CARTER, ALFRED, petitioned for the estate of Woodroffe Sinclair Carter on 25 September 1825. [The Barbadian iii]

CARTER, BENJAMIN, an apprentice in Bridewell, bound for Barbados in 1632. [Bridewell Court Minutes]

CARTER, ELINOR, from Barbados aboard the Joseph and Ann, master Samuel Evans, bound for Carolina on 7 January 1679. [TNA]

CARTER, Reverend JOHN, MA, died on 21 October 1796. [St George's MI]

CARTER, Captain, of the Mail Boat Service married Miss King, daughter of James S. King on 27 October 1825. [The Barbadian iii]

CARVALHO, DANIEL, in Bridgetown, 1772. [BDA.Levy]

CARVALHO, RACHEL, in Bridgetown, 1772. [BDA.Levy]

CARY, RICHARD, from Barbados aboard the pink Sea Venture, master George Battersby, bound for Antigua on 10 March 1679. [TNA]

CASTELLO, DAVID NUNES, in Bridgetown, 1772. [BDA.Levy]

CAVAN, MICHAEL, born 1780, a merchant, died in Barbados on 6 June 1832. [GM.102.94]; of the firm of J. and M. Cavan, announced his intention to move to London in April 1825. [The Barbadian iii]

CAVE, JOHN, born 1790, second son of Stephen Cave in Clevehill, Bristol, died in Barbados on 18 January 1808. [GM.78.364]

CAWCATT, SARAH, a spinster from Laniger, Gloucestershire, an indentured servant bound for Barbados in November 1659. [Gloucestershire Record Office. C.10/2]

CAWFIELD, RICHARD, from Barbados aboard the Young William, master Thomas Cornish, bound for Virginia in 28 July 1679. [TNA]

CHALLENOR, ROBERT, sr., born 12 October 1809, a merchant in Speight's Town, died 25 August 1876. [St Peter's, Speight's Town, MI]

CHALLENOR, THOMAS, born 1776, died 10 May 1840, husband of Margaret Bend, born 1781, died 9 October 1845. [St Peter's, Speight's Town, MI]

CHAMBERLAIN, Colonel EDWARD, born 1623 in Leicestershire, a Councillor of Barbados, husband of Mary Butler, died 23 July 1673. [St Michael's MI]; a merchant in Barbados, was appointed attorney for George Seignior a barber surgeon of London in 1658. [CLRO.M8]

CHAMBERLAIN, JEREMIAH, from Barbados aboard the Joseph and Ann, master Samuel Evans, bound for Carolina on 7 January 1679. [TNA]

CHAMBERLAINE, MARMADUKE, from Barbados aboard the Endeavour, master James Gilbert, bound for London on 1 April 1679. [TNA]

CHAPLIN, THOMAS, from Barbados aboard the Maligo Merchant, master Roger Horner, bound for London on 22 September 1679. [TNA]

CHAPMAN, BENJAMIN, born 29 September 1857, son of Peter and Mary Emlin Chapman, died 6 March 1859. [St Michael's MI]

CHAPMAN, J. T., died 1 April 1852. [Christ Church MI]

CHARINGTON, ..., and family, a planter in Barbados, returned aboard the Polly and Charlotte, from Portsmouth to Barbados in March 1776. [TNA.T47.9/11]

CHARLES, EVAN, from Barbados aboard the sloop True Friendship, master Charles Callahan, bound for Antigua on 6 October 1679. [TNA]

CHARNOCK, JOHN, born 1722, from Barbados, died in Bath on 16 July 1809. [GM.79.686]

CHASE, JOHN, born 1704, died 9 February 1736, husband of Christian, parents of John born 1736, died 11 April 1737. [Christ Church MI]

CHASE, THOMAS J., married Joyce Bristow in June 1825. [The Barbadian iii]

CHAVASSE, ARABELLA, born 4 April 1816, died 3 April 1851, wife of Nathaniel Forte. [St Thomas MI]

CHEARNLEY, MARY, wife of Captain Edward Chearnley, died 3 December 1723. [St Michael's MI]

CHEEKS, HENRY, born 1749, died 25 December 1824. [St Michael's MI]

CHEESMAN, HENRY, born 1800, died 8 December 1844. [St Michael's MI]

CHESTER, SAMPSON, from Barbados aboard the Malaga Merchant, master Roger Horner, bound for London on 20 September 1679. [TNA]

CHETWYND, WALTER, a Member of Parliament and Governor of Barbados, died on 4 February 1732. [GM.2.630]

CHILTON, EDWARD, in Barbados, probate, 28 July 1707, PCC. [TNA.Prob.11.495.367]

CHOLMLEY, Mrs, widow of Robert Cholmley in Barbados, married Thomas Workman, in Barbados in 1757. [GM.27.530]

CLARKE, ANN, from Barbados aboard the Samuel, bound for London on 1 March 1679. [TNA]

CLARK, ELIZABETH, third daughter of Sir Bowcher Clark the Chief Justice of Barbados, married Captain Dugald Stewart Miller, Quartermaster of the 67th Regiment, eldest son of Dr Miller in Exeter, in Barbados on 20 May 1858. [GM.ns.2/5.185]

CLARKE, EMILY SPOONER, eldest daughter of Sir R B Clarke, the Chief Justice of Barbados, married Charles Edward Mitchel, a Major of the 66t Regiment, in Barbados on 19 November 1850. [GM.ns.35.196]

CLARKE, FORSTER, born 1777, died 2 January 1840, Member of HM Council of Barbados. [St George's MI]

CLARKE, MARY, from Barbados aboard the Experiment, master Alan Cock, bound for London on 10 May 1679. [TNA]

CLARKE, NATHANIEL, in Bridewell, an apprentice bound for Barbados in 1632. [Bridewell Court Minutes]

CLARKE, PORCAS, from Barbados aboard the Supply, master Joseph Freeman, bound for London on 24 March 1679. [TNA]

CLARK, RICHARD, born 1614, bound from London aboard the Hopewell to Barbados in February 1635. [TNA.E157.20]

CLARKE, SAMUEL T., of Spencer's Plantation, died in Barbados on 3 September 1837. [GM.ns.9.222]

CLARKE, Mrs SARAH, died in January 1825. [The Barbadian iii]

CLARKE, SILVESTER, married Catherine Ann Frederick, in St Michael's Cathedral in September 1825. [The Barbadian iii]

CLARKE, THOMAS WILTSHIRE, born 1753, died on 1 August 1825. [The Barbadian iii]

CLAYPOOL, JOHN, from Barbados aboard the Patience, master Thomas Hudson, bound for London on 5 March 1679. [TNA]

CLAYPOOLE, NORTON, from Barbados aboard the Bachelor's Delight, master Robert Greenway, bound for New York on 22 February 1679. [TNA]

CLEWER, JOHN, a bachelor in Barbados, Admin., 1650, PCC

CLINCKETT, ABEL, born 1775, died 1854, husband of Mary Judith, born 1788, died 1862. [St Michael's MI]

CLINKETT, Reverend G M Clinkett of St Matthew's, Claremont, son of Abel Clinkett in Barbados, married Jane Henry, youngest daughter of Reverend William Henry of Tooting, Surrey, in Jamaica on 10 January 1851. [GM.ns.35.545]

CLINKETT, MARY ABEL, born 1798, daughter of Abel Clinkett of Barbados, wife of Alfred Bartrum of Mauritius, died 5 April 1830, parents of Ellen Pringle Bartrum, born 1817, died 16 June 1834. [St Michael's MI]

CLINKETT, REBECCA HOWELL, daughter of Abel Clinkett, was born in Barbados on 29 December 1823. [The Barbadian.ii]

CLINTON, ELIZABETH, petitioned for the estate of Peter Lawton on 15 November 1825. [The Barbadian iii]

CLYNTON, RICHARD, born 1612, bound from London aboard the Hopewell to Barbados in February 1635. [TNA.E157.20]

CLOETE, Sir ABRAHAM JOSIAS, Commanding Officer of the Windward Islands and Demerara, married Anne Woollcombe, eldest daughter of Thomas Louis of Culloden, Barbados, and granddaughter of Rear Admiral Sir Thomas Bent, in Cadwell, Barbados, on 8 July 1857. [GM.ns.2/3.328]

CLOVAN, THOMAS, from Barbados aboard the sloop <u>True Friendship,</u> master Charles Callahan, bound for Nevis on 31 May 1679. [TNA]

CLOVAN, THOMAS, from Barbados aboard the sloop <u>True Friendship,</u> master Charles Callahan, bound for Antigua on 2 October 1679. [TNA]

COBHAM, FRANCIS, MD, born1798, died in Barbados on 29 May 1831. [GM.101.94]

COBHAM, RICHARD, was appointed a Councillor of Barbados in 1772. [PC.Col.V.562]

COBHAM, RICHARD, Judge of the Vice Admiralty Court, married Katherine Anne Hinds, daughter of Richard Skinner, in Barbados on 30 March 1819. [GM.88.480]

COCKERALL, BENJAMIN, died in Bridgetown in July 1824. [The Barbadian.ii]

CODD, JOHN MORSE, third son of Captain Codd of the War Office, died in Barbados on 1 October 1809. [GM.79.1174]

COLE, JAMES, from Barbados aboard the sloop <u>John and Francis,</u> master John Howard, bund for Antigua on 2 September 1679. [TNA]

COLE, JOHN, a tailor from Worcester, an indentured servant, bound via Bristol for Barbados in 1660. [BRO]

COLE, THOMAS, jr, from Barbados aboard the <u>Prevention,</u> master Bernard Booghert, bound for Surinam on 1 July 1679. [TNA]

COLEBROOK, EMMA SOPHIA, wife of Sir William Colebrooke, a Colonel in the Royal Artillery, Governor of the Windward Islands, died in Barbados on 18 April 1851. [GM.ns.36.99]

COLEMAN, J G, Deputy Naval Officer of Barbados, died on passage from Trinidad to St Kitts on 24 January 1810. [GM.80.491]

COLERIDGE, GEORGINA BLACKSTONE, infant daughter of Reverend W H Coleridge, the Bishop of Barbados, died in Devon on29 September 1835. [GM.ns4.556]

COLLE, FRANCIS, born 1749, a carpenter from Hertfordshire, 'going as a surveyor' via London aboard the Richmond, bound for Barbados in December 1774. [TNA.T47.9/11]

COLLETON, Captain PETER, a merchant in Barbados, attorney for Hugh Sowden a merchant in London, 1660. [CLRO.Deposition.10]

COLLETON, THOMAS, a merchant in Barbados, attorney for Hugh Sowden a merchant in London, 1660. [CLRO.Deposition.10]

COLLIER, THOMAS, a merchant in Barbados, attorney for Elizabeth Swift relict of William Swift late master of the Benjamin of London, 1660. [CLRO.Deposition.10]

COLLIER, WILLIAM, in Barbados, married Miss Warren of Wotton, Berkshire, on 18 September 1760. [GM.30.490]

COLLINS, JOHN, from Barbados in the ketch Neptune, master Joseph Knott, bound for Carolina on 2 July 1679. [TNA]

COLLINS, JOHN, from Barbados in the barque Plantation, master Aser Sharpe, bound for Carolina on 9 August 1679. [TNA]

COLLIS, ALEXANDER, from Barbados aboard the Hope, master John Price, bound for New England on 18 September 1679. [TNA]

COLLYER, AMBROSE, from Barbados aboard the pink Society, master William Guard, bound for Boston on 11 March 1679. [TNA]

COLLYMORE, JOHN, son of Henry Collymore, a druggist, died in October 1825. [The Barbadian iii]

COLLYMORE, ROBERT, of Haggatt Hall, died on 7 May 1824. [The Barbadian.ii]

COLTHROUGH, PETER, from Barbados aboard the Samuel and Eliza, master Thomas Orchard, bound for Londonderry on 25 April 1679. [TNA]

COLTON, ..., a planter in Barbados, returned aboard the Three Brothers, from Portsmouth to Barbados in March 1776. [TNA.T47.9/11]

COLWELL, SAMUEL, from Barbados aboard the ketch William and Susan, master Ralph Parker, bound for New England on 21 March 1679. [TNA]

COMB, WILLIAM, from Hatherleigh, Devon, an indentured servant bound via Bristol for Barbados in December 1658. [BRO]

COMBERBATCH, ABRAHAM, was appointed a Councillor of Barbados in 1780. [PC.Col.V.563]

CONNELL, HOWARD, married Rebecca, second daughter of John Wickham, on 21 April 1825. [The Barbadian iii]

CONNELL, MARY, petitioned for the estate of late William Connell in June 1825. [The Barbadian iii]

CONNELL, THOMAS, born 1771, died 22 September 1846, husband of Elizabeth ......, born 1774, died 12 July 1827. [St Lucy's gravestone]

CONNELL, Reverend THOMAS GRIFFITH, of Barbados, married Maria Jane, widow of John P Oyer of Barbados, in Windsor on 1 September 1853. [GM.ns.40.626]

COOK, JOHN, an inkhorn maker, from London aboard the Elizabeth of London, from London to Barbados in 1658. [CLRO.Deposition.9]

COOKE, JOHN, a merchant in Barbados, attorney for John Jekyll a fishmonger in London, 1660. [CLRO.Deposition.10]

COOK, MARY, wife of Assistant Commissary General Cook, died in Barbados on 27 October 1811. [GM.82.488]

COOPER, MARY, a servant of Robert Daniel, from Barbados aboard the Mary, master Nicholas Lockwood, bound for Carolina on 3 April 1679. [TNA]

COOPER, REGINALD, in Barbados, probate, 12 October 1749. [TNA.Prob.774.110]

COOPER, THOMAS, from Barbados aboard the pink Blessing, master John Thwing, bound for New York, on 6 March 1679. [TNA]

COOPER, TOBIAS, died in Barbados, Admin., 1655, PCC

CORBETT, WILLIAM, from Barbados aboard the sloop Katherine, master Andrew Gall, bound for Antigua on 27 October 1679. [TNA]

CORDOZA, SOLOMAN, with three children, in St Michael's, Barbados, in 1680. [HOT.450]

CORNELIUS, FRANCIS, from Barbados aboard the barque Joseph, master Stephen Clay, bound for 'Saltertudos' on 21 March 1679. [TNA]

CORNISH, EDWARD, a servant of John Harris, from Barbados aboard the William and John, master Samuel Legg, bound for Boston on 28 May 1679. [TNA]

COSTANAO, ABRAHAM, with two children, in St Michael's, Barbados, in 1680. [HOT.450]

COTINHO, MOSES HENRIQUES, from Barbados aboard the barque Adventure, master Edward Duffield, bound for Antigua on 3 November 1679. [TNA]

COTTINGHAM, KATHERINE, from Barbados aboard the Eliza, master Sylvanus Paine, bound for Jamaica on 2 August 1679. [TNA]

COTTON, DUDLEY PAGE, died 30 July 1880. [St Leonard's MI]

COULBURNE, JOHN, from Barbados aboard the Conclusion, master William Beeding, bound for London on 22 May 1679. [TNA]

COULTHURST, ELIZABETH, wife of Matthew Coulthurst in Barbados, died on 12 October 1820. [GM.90.473]

COULTHURST, MATTHEW, born 30 September 1757, died 24 June 1833. [St Michael's MI]; resigned as Attorney General on 21 September 1824. [The Barbadian ii]

COURTNEY, WILLIAM, from Barbados aboard the sloop Hopewell, master William Murphy, bound for Antigua on 7 November 1679. [TNA]

COWCAM, ELIZABETH, a spinster from Newland, Gloucestershire, an indentured servant bound for Barbados in November 1659. [Gloucestershire Record Office. C.10/2]

COWLEY, ABRAHAM, in Barbados, probate, 5 January 1706, PCC. [TNA.Prob.11.486.49]

COX, FRANCIS, from Barbados aboard the John and James, master Giles Hamlin, bound for New England on 25 August 1679. [TNA]

COX, MARGARET MATTHEWS, wife of James William Cox of Rising Sun Plantation, Barbados, in 1829, daughter of Thomas Le Gall and his wife Hannah Best. [BDA.171.535.38]

COX, ROBERT, of Barbados, died in Westminster, Admin., 1652, PCC

COX, THOMAS G., died at Rockley, Christ Church, on 2 January 1824. [The Barbadian.ii]

COX, Mrs, a widow, died at the residence of George Moe in March 1824. [The Barbadian.ii]

CRAGG, JOHN, from Barbados aboard the ketch Friendship, master Joseph Hardy, bound for New England on 30 January 1679. [TNA]

CRAGG, THOMAS, arrived in Bridgetown aboard the Mercy in February 1825. [The Barbadian iii]; born 1786, died in Barbados on 18 May 1825. [The Barbadian iii]

CRANE, WILLIAM, born 1787, purser aboard HMS Sapphire died 10 December 1833. [St Michael's MI]

CRANFIELD, EDWARD, in Barbados, Admin., 1649, PCC

CRANFIELD, EDWARD, who died in Barbados, Admin., 1658, PCC

CRANFEILD, FRANCIS, in Barbados, eldest son and heir to Edward Cranfield of London, probate, 1656, PCC

CRAWFORD, Reverend Sir George W Crawford, married Martha Cooke, widow of William Cooke of Burgh House, Lincoln, in Barbados on 3 May 1849. [GM.ns.32.84]

CRICHLOW, WILLIAM, eldest son of Charles Crichlow of Barbados, married Martha Bailie, eldest daughter of Robert Bailie of Belfast, in Edmonton, London, on 4 February 1825. [Barbadian iii]

CRILLICK, JANE, a servant belonging to John Follit, from Barbados aboard the Old Head of Kinsale, master Robert Barker, bound for the Leeward Islands on 4 January 1679. [TNA]

CRISP, EDWARD, born 1628, son of Nicholas Crisp a merchant in Bread Street, London, a merchant in Barbados, died 14 January 1678. [St Michael's MI]

CRISP, ROGER, from Barbados aboard the Ann and Jane, master Richard Radford, bound for London on 5 December 1679. [TNA]

CROCKER, ..., son of Surgeon Major Alfred Crocker, was born in Barbados on 5 August 1864. [GM.ns.2/17.510]

CROFT, Miss, eldest daughter of Sir Arthur Croft in Barbados, married James Woodcock of Jamaica in 1777. [GM.48.237]

CROMARTIE, CONSTANCE EDWARDS, second daughter of F M Cromartie the Deputy Superintendent of Military Stores, married Richard William Charles Winsloe, Captain of the 21st Royal North British Fusiliers, in Barbados on 12 September 1861. [GM.ns.2/11.557]

CROMARTIE, EDWARD, arrived in Bridgetown aboard the Renewal in February 1825, from London. [The Barbadian iii]

CROMARTIE, MATTHEW, arrived in Bridgetown aboard the Renewal in February 1825, from London. [The Barbadian iii]; he married Charlotte Lloyd, daughter of William Draper Lloyd on 16 August 1824. [The Barbadian ii]

CROOKENDEN, MARY, a widow in Barbados, probate, 16 June 1824, PCC. [TNA.Prob.11.1686.383]

CROSBY, Reverend S. Oliver of St Philips, Barbados, married Catherine, third daughter of Reverend John Warneford of Caldicott Hill, Hertfordshire, in Barbados on 30 May 1848. [GM.ns.30.314]

CROSSING, WILLIAM, from Barbados aboard the Blessing, master Samuel Richard, bound for Boston on 1 April 1679. [TNA]

CROUCH, Mrs ELIZABETH, born 1695, died 30 May 1747. [St Michael's MI]

CUMBERBATCH, EDWARD ARNOLD, of Barbados, married Mary Gertrude, daughter of A. Ashe of Belvidere, in Bath on 6 August 1822. [GM.92.178]

CUMMINS, CHARLES CRICHLOW, married Mary Fitzpatrick, in Worthing in July 1824. [The Barbadian ii]; parents of a daughter born in May 1825. [The Barbadian iii]

CUMMINS, JOHN ASHLEY, born 1819, Deputy Assistant General, died in Barbados on 1 January 1853. [GM.ns.39.448]

CUMMINS, NORMAN J D, born 1862, organist and choirmaster, died 3 April 1887. [St Michael's MI]

CUMMINS, Mrs, widow of the Quartermaster General of Barbados, and daughter of Baron de Bretton in St Croix, died in St Anne's, Barbados, on 12 July 1821. [GM.91.283]

CUNNINGHAM, REBECCA ANNE, wife of C T Cunningham the Colonial Secretary, died in Barbados on 2 August 1837. [GM.ns.8.551]

CUPPAGE, Captain ADAM, born 1794, Justice of Barbados, died there on 14 February 1859. [GM.ns.2/6.56]

CUPPAGE, MARGARET HUGHES, only daughter of Judge Adam Cuppage, married John Hampden King an Assemblyman and a barrister, in Barbados on 30 October 1850. [GM.ns.35.195]

CURLE, HENRY, from Barbados, married Marianne Ellen Tillett, second daughter of John Edward Tillett from Liverpool, in London on 23 December 1848. [GM.ns.31.311]

CURREY, JOHN, from Barbados, died in London on 19 December 1770. [GM.40.591]

CURTIS, JOHN, from Barbados aboard the Concord, master James Strutt, bound for London on 3 May 1679. [TNA]

CUTTING, JOHN H., MD, married Mary Williams, daughter of James Thomas Williams, at the Hill, St George, on 6 December 1824. [The Barbadian ii]

DA COSTA, MOSES MENDES, born 1780, died in Barbados on 8 November 1845. [GM.ns.24.665]

DANG, MARGARET, from Barbados aboard the sloop Resolution, master John Ingleby, bound for Nevis on 14 February 1679. [TNA]

DANGERFIELD, THOMAS, an indentured servant bound via Bristol for Barbados in December 1658. [BRO]

DANGERFIELD, WALCUP, from Barbados aboard the Bachelor, master Roger Bagg, bound for Bristol on 14 May 1679. [TNA]

DANIELL, JOHN, from Barbados aboard the barque John's Adventure, master John Welch, bound for Antigua on 9 April 1679. [TNA]

DANIELL, ROBERT, from Barbados, aboard the Mary, master Nicholas Lockwood, bound for Carolina on 4 April 1679. [TNA]

DANIELL, WILBERT, from Barbados aboard the Supply, master John Ady, bound for Virginia on 27 September 1679. [TNA]

DARRELL, SUSAN MATILDA, second daughter of Thomas Darrell in Barbados, married John McArthur of Bristol, in Clifton on 8 September 1842. [GM.ns.18.651]

DAVIES, ELIZA, a servant of Hlliard Holdip, from Barbados aboard the London Merchant, master Edward Desworth, bound for London on 22 April 1679. [TNA]

DAVIES, JANE, a servant of Richard Townsend, from Barbados aboard the Nathaniel, master William Clarke, bound for Boston on 28 April 1679. [TNA]

DAVIES, JOHN, jr., from Barbados aboard the Roebuck, master William Shafto, bound for London on 13 May 1679. [TNA]

DAVIES, JOHN, from Barbados aboard the Coast Frigate, master Philip Varlos, bound for London on 11 June 1679. [TNA]

DAVIES, JOHN, from Christ Church, Barbados, aboard the ketch Joseph, master Abraham Knott, bound for New York on 11 June 1679. [TNA]

DAVIES, KATHERINE, a servant of John Austin, from Barbados aboard the Young William, master Thomas Cornish, bound for Virginia on 2 August 1679. [TNA]

DAVIES, PETER, from Barbados aboard the pink Neptune, master Joseph Knott, bound for Carolina on 21 June 1679. [TNA]

DAVIES, SAMUEL, from Barbados aboard the ketch Prosperous, master David Fogg, bound for Virginia on 2 May 1679. [TNA]

DAVIS, ALICE, a widow from Hereford, an indentured servant bound via Bristol for Barbados in December 1658. [BRO]

DAVIS, HENRY, son of Charles Davis in Derby, an indentured servant bound via Liverpool for Barbados in 1698. [LRO]

PEOPLE OF BARBADOS, 1625-1875

DAWSON, CHRISTOPHER, died in Barbados, Admin. 1660, PCC

DAWSON, TREMMIT, from Barbados aboard the _Eliza,_ master Silvanus Payne, bound for Jamaica on 2 August 1679. [TNA]

DAY, JOHN, a bachelor, died in Barbados, Admin., 1658, PCC

DAVY, ROBERT, from Barbados aboard the _Ann and Jane,_ master Richard Ratford, bound for London on 24 December 1679. [TNA]

DAY, WILLIAM, a gentleman in St Michael's, Barbados, probate, 24 July 1751, PCC. [TNA.Prob.11.789.227]

DAY, WILLOUGHBY, born 1760, a lad from London, via London aboard the _Britannia,_ bound for Barbados in October 1774. [TNA.T47.9/11]

DAYES, THOMAS, born 1615, bound from London aboard the _Hopewell_ to Barbados in February 1635. [TNA.E157.20]

DAYRELL, MARY ELVIRA, daughter of Thomas Dayrell in Barbados, died in England on 6 April 1825. [The Barbadian iii]

DEANE, FRANCES, petitioned for the estate of her husband John Gibson Deane on 13 September 1825. [The Barbadian iii]

DECHAUIS, SAMUEL, with two children, in St Michael's, Barbados, in 1680. [HOT.450]

DE COMPAS, Mrs LEAH, with three children, in St Michael's, Barbados, in 1680. [HOT.449]

DE COSTA, BENJAMIN, in Bridgetown, 1772. [BDA.Levy]

DE CRASTO, LIAH, in Bridgetown, 1772. [BDA.Levy]

DE CRASTO, RACHEL, in Bridgetown, 1772. [BDA.Levy]

DEED, THOMAS, a smith from Bristol, an indentured servant bound via Bristol for Barbados in December 1658. [BRO]

DE LAGAL, ELIZABETH, born 1748, widow of Henry Sacheverall De Lagal in Barbados, died in London on 4 January 1811. [GM.81.88]

DELLON, AARON, in Bridgetown, 1772. [BDA.Levy]

DELLON, ABIGAIL, in Bridgetown, 1772. [BDA.Levy]

DEMEREADO, DAVID RAPLH, with three children, in St Michael's, Barbados, in 1680. [HOT.449]; died 14 August 1685. [Bridgetown gravestone]; probate, 9 December 1685, PCC.

DENSY, JANE, from Barbados aboard the Hope, master Joseph Ball, bound for London on 22 April 1679. [TNA]

DENTON, JOHN, from Barbados aboard the Endeavour, master Abraham Newman, bound for Virginia on 21 February 1679. [TNA]

DE PAZ, MOSES, in Bridgetown, 1772. [BDA.Levy]

DE PIZA, ANGEL, born 1747, wife of Emanuel a merchant, died 12 March 1795. [Bridgetown gravestone]

DE PIZA, EMMANUEL. in Bridgetown, 1772. [BDA.Levy]

DE PIZA, ISAAC, in Bridgetown, 1772. [BDA. Levy]

DE PIA, MOSES, in Bridgetown, 1772. [BDA.Levy]

DE SAGULIERS, GABRIEL, in Barbados, died in 1768. [GM.38.198]

DE SALANEUVE, Captain PETER, of Weymouth, Dorset, with property in Barbados, probate 1655, PCC

DESAUIDO, MOSES, with five children, in St Michael's, Barbados, in 1680. [HOT.450]

DEUREDE, PAUL, with two children, in St Michael's, Barbados, in 1680. [HOT.449]

DEVENISH, JOHN, from Barbados aboard the Endeavour, master James Gilbert, bound for London on 20 March 1679. [TNA]

DEWAR, STEPHEN, from Barbados aboard the barque Resolution, master Thomas Gilbert, bound for Antigua on 15 November 1679. [TNA]

DE WEVER, LEWIN, from Barbados, aboard the Blossom, master Richard Martin, bound for Surinam on 24 December 1679. [TNA]

DEXTER, WILLIAM, from Barbados aboard the Ann and Jane, master Richard Ratford, bound for London on 15 December 1679. [TNA]

DIAS, LEWIS, with six children, in St Michael's, Barbados, in 1680. [HOT.449]

DIAS, LUIS, in Barbados, born 1613, died 27 December 1699, [Bridgetown gravestone]; probate, 4 February 1706, [TNA.Prob.11.486.347]

DICKENSON, FRANCIS, from Barbados aboard the Blessing, bound for Boston on 1 April 1679. [TNA]

DICKENSON, WILLIAM, died in Barbados, Admin. 1660, PCC

DOLDRON, GRACE, from Barbados aboard the Samuel, master John Clarke, bound for London on 1 March 1679. [TNA]

DOLEBERRY, ANDREW, from Barbados aboard the Society, master William Guard, bound for Boston on 10 March 1679. [TNA]

DOLLMAN, ROBERT, a merchant in Barbados, purchased a share in the Elizabeth of London in 1658. [CLRO.Deposition,9]

DOTTIN, JOHN, was appointed a Councillor of Barbados in 1780. [PC.Col.V.563]

DOUSE, BRIDGETT, from Barbados aboard the Ann and Jane, master Richard Ratford, bound for London on 22 December 1679. [TNA]

DOWELL, DENNIS, from Barbados aboard the Industry, master James Porter, bound for Bristol on 12 May 1679. [TNA]

DOWNIE, M., from Demerara, died in Barbados on 17 May 1818. [GM.88.87]

DOWNING, JOHN, from Barbados aboard the Laurel, master Robert Ox, bound for Nevis on 22 December 1679. [TNA]

DRAN, MAREN, a servant of Jacob Le Roux, from Barbados aboard the ketch Dove, master John Grafton, bound for Antigua on 29 June 1679. [TNA]

DRAX, HENRY, from Barbados aboard the Thomas Warren, master Warren, bound for London on 22 April 1679. [TNA]

DRAYTON, JOHN, of Mollineux Plantation, born 1794, died 11 January 1849, husband of Rebecca Jane Drayton. [St Thomas gravestone]

DRAYTON, THOMAS, jr., from Barbados aboard the Mary, master Nicholas Lockwood, bound for Carolina on 25 April 1679. [TNA]

DRAYTON, WILLIAM, from Barbados, died in London on 26 December 1846. [GM.ns.27.214]

DU BOYES, JOHN, from Barbados aboard the Supply, master John Mellowes, bound for Boston on 24 May 1679. [TNA]

DUKE, Mrs ELIZABETH A., widow of General Duke, died on 19 June 1825. [The Barbadian iii]

DUKES, WILLIAM, from Barbados aboard the barque Adventure, master Daniel Ridley, bound for Carolina on 7 April 1679. [TNA]

DUNDAS, WILLIAM, from Barbados aboard the Young William, master Thomas Cornish, bound for Virginia on 1 August 1679. [TNA]

DUNN, JOHN, a bachelor, died in Barbados, Admin., 1655, PCC

DUNN, Mrs MARGARET ANN, born 1786, died 19 February 1829. [St Michael's MI]

DUNNAHOE, CORNELIUS, from Barbados aboard the Margaret, master Alexander Wood, bound for Beaumorris on 11 June 1679. [TNA]

DUNNAHOE, JEFFREY, from Barbados aboard the Margaret, master Alexander Wood, bound for Beaumorris on 11 June 1679. [TNA]

DUNNAHOE, TAAG, from Barbados aboard the Margaret, master Alexander Wood, bound for Beaumorris on 23 May 1679. [TNA]

DUNSTER, GILES, a merchant from London, settled in Barbados by December 1659. [CLRO.Deposition.9]

DYMOND, ROBERT, born 1606, bound from London aboard the Hopewell to Barbados in February 1635. [TNA.E157.20]

EARLE, JOHN, from Barbados aboard the Defiance, master William Creed, bound for London on 26 April 1679. [TNA]

EASTCHURCH, WILLIAM, from Barbados aboard the Joseph, bound for London on 26 July 1679. [TNA]

EASTON, CHARLES, a merchant in Barbados, probate, 1646, PCC

EATON, JOHN, born 1615, bound from London aboard the Hopewell to Barbados in February 1635. [TNA.E157.20]

EDWARDS, DAVID, from Penterk, an indentured servant bound via Bristol for Barbados in December 1658. [BRO]

EDWARDS, JOHN, from Barbados aboard the Society, bound for Bristol on 28 April 1679. [TNA]

EDWARDS, WILLIAM, a planter in Barbados, died in Plymouth, Devon, probate, 23.12.1645, PCC, [TNA.Prob.11.194.505]

EGGINTON, JEREMY, a merchant in Barbados, an attorney there in November 1659. [CLRO.Deposition.9]

EIRKETT, Mrs ELIZABETH, died on 27 October 1825. [The Barbadian iii]

ELDER, JOHN W. K. E., attorney at law, died at Worthing in September 1825. [The Barbadian iii]

ELKIN, ISAAC JOSEPH, infant son of Mozley Elkin, died on 19 March 1824. [The Barbadian. ii]

ELKIN, MOZELY, married Sarah Lindo, daughter of David Lindo, in Bridgetown in March 1825. [The Barbadian iii]

ELLCOCK, REYNOLD ALLEYNE, born 1789, died 2 October 1821. [St Thomas MI]

ELLCOCK, Mrs, widow of Grant Ellcock, MD, died in December 1824. [The Barbadian ii]

ELLICOTT, VINES, from Barbados aboard the Supply, master John Mellowes, bound for Boston on 24 May 1679. [TNA]

ELLINSWORTH, WILLIAM, from Barbados aboard the pink Portsmouth, master Joseph Briar, bound for Rhode Island on 2 October 1679. [TNA]

ELLIOTT, GEORGE, died bound for Barbados, Admin., Admin., 1658, PCC

ELLIOTT, HENRY, from Barbados aboard the True Friendship, master Charles Callahan, bound for Antigua on 2 October 1679. [TNA]

ELLIOT, JAMES, born 1690, son of Richard Elliot, husband of Elizabeth Walrond, died 14 May 1724. [Christ Church MI]

ELLIS, JOHN, born 19 January 1791, a barrister, died 24 May 1825. [St Michael's MI]; born 19 January 1791, a barrister at Law, son of John Ellis of the Stock Exchange, died on 24 May 1825. [The Barbadian iii]

ELLIS, JOHN BRYANTE, born 1845, died 3 August 1869, son of Thomas Ellis. [St Thomas MI]

ELLIS, RICHARD, a bachelor who died in Barbados, Admin., 1658, PCC

ELLIS, WILLIAM GRANT, born 1782, died 10 January 1841. [St Thomas MI]

ELLIS, WILLIAM BRIAN, born 1 January 1821, son of John Thomas Ellis, died 2 December 1854. [St Thomas MI]

ELLISTON, GEORGE, from Barbados aboard the Nathaniel, master William Clarke, bound for Boston on 26 April 1679. [TNA]

ELSON, WILLIAM, from Barbados aboard the ketch Beginning, master William Play, bound for New York on 20 March 1679. [TNA]

EMBLEN, WILLIAM, a merchant in Barbados, probate, 8 November 1677. [TNA.Prob.11.355.246]

EMERY, JOHN, a servant of Lieutenant Colonel Hallett, from Barbados aboard the Young William, master Thomas Cornish, bound for Virginia on 31 July1679. [TNA]

ENDERBEE, OLIVER, from Barbados aboard the Ann and Mary, master John Johnson, bound for Antigua on 13March 1679. [TNA]

ESTON, THOMAS and JAMES, Bristol merchants trading with Barbados, 1661-1688. [BRO.ms16163]

ESTWICK, ELIZABETH, born 1754, died in January 1825, buried in St Michael's, sister of R. J. Estwick and of Samuel Estwick, the Barbados Colonial Agent in London. [The Barbadian iii]

ESTWICK, ELIZABETH, born 1715, daughter of Christopher Estwick and his wife Elizabeth, died 17 June 1732. [St John's MI]

ESTWICK, RICHARD JAMES, was appointed a Councillor of Barbados in 1782. [PC.Col.V.563]

ESTWICK, ..., a gentleman of Barbados, via Portsmouth aboard the Favourite Betsey, bound for Barbados in April 1774. [TNA.T47.9/11]

EVANS, EDWARD, from Barbados aboard the pink Neptune, master Joseph Knott, bound for Carolina on 21 June1679. [TNA]

EVANS, LEWIS, from Barbados aboard the ketch Unity, master James Rainy, bound for Virginia on 25 April 1679. [TNA]

EVANS, THOMAS, born 1748, a servant from London, via London aboard the Britannia, bound for Barbados in October 1774. [TNA.T47.9/11]

EVANS, WILLIAM, bound from Barbados aboard the William and Robert, master Giles Bond, bound for London on 20 June1679. [TNA]

EVELYN, CHARLES, died in Christ Church in January 1825. [The Barbadian iii]

EVERSLEY, EDMUND, born 1750, died in October 1824. [The Barbadian ii]

EVERSLEY, ELIZABETH, born 1781, wife of William Eversley, died 6 October 1817. [Christ Church MI]

EVERSLEY, JOHN CHASE, was appointed Episcopal Registrar of the Diocese of Barbados and the Leeward Islands on 13 July 1825. [The Barbadian iii]

EVERSLEY, ..., 'the lady and daughter of William Eversley' arrived in Barbados from London aboard the Tropic from London in July 1824. [The Barbadian.ii]

EVERSLEY, ..., son of Edmund J. Eversley, was born in December 1824. [The Barbadian ii]

EVERSLEY, ..., daughter of John C. Eversley, was born at Windsor Lodge in September 1825. [The Barbadian iii]

EVERSON, GEORGE, witness to a deed subscribed in St Michael's, Barbados, on 28 June 1749. [NRS.RD4.177/1.397]

FABOR, FREDERICK, from London, died in Barbados, Admin., 1649, PCC

FAIRCHILD, JOHN, Chief Justice in St Michael's, Barbados, died on 12 September 1757. [GM.27.46]

FALCON, Reverend THOMAS, MA, Fellow of Queens College, Oxford, and Master of Codrington College in Barbados, born 1729, died 4 February 1762. [St George's MI]

FALKLAND, CHARLES, petitioned for the estate of Isaac Depiza Massiah, on 13 May 1825. [The Barbadian iii]

FANING, ANDREW, a servant of Daniel Stanton, from Barbados aboard the Diligence, master Gev. Jackson, bound for New England on 6 February 1679. [TNA]

FARLEY, Mrs ELEANOR, born 1693, wife of Isaac Farley in Berbice, died 11 July 1823. [St Michael's MI]

FARMER, ROGER, a gentleman in St James, Barbados, probate, 1649, PCC,

FARNUM, Miss ELIZABETH, of Bridgetown, died in May 1824. [The Barbadian.ii]

FARNUM, RICHARD, married Miss Greenidge, in St Michael's church on 1 March 1824. [The Barbadian. ii]

FARRELL, CHRISTOPHER, from Barbados aboard the Ann and Jane, master Richard Ratford, bound for London on 22 December 1679. [TNA]

FARRELL, HUGH, from Barbados aboard the barque Dove, master Anthony Jenour, bound for Nevis on 29 October 1679. [TNA]

FARRELL, JOHN RICHARD, of Barbados, died at Lamplighter Hall on 30 December 1824. [GM.95.189]; his wife Elizabeth Farrell, born 1749, died 18 June 1819. [Christ Church MI]

FARRELL, ROGER, from Barbados aboard the sloop Katherine, master Andrew Gall bound for Antigua on 26 November 1679. [TNA]

FARROR, EDMOND, from Barbados aboard the Ann and Jane, master Richard Ratford, bound for London on 24 December 1679. [TNA]

FARRER, JAMES, from Barbados aboard the Conclusion, master William Beeding, bound for London on 26 May 1679. [TNA]

FEAGHERY, THOMAS, from Barbados aboard the John and Thomas, master Thomas Jenour, bound for Providence on 6 May 1679. [TNA]

FELL, LIDIA, from Barbados aboard the ketch John and Sarah, master Peter Carew, bound for New York on 11 June 1679. [TNA]

FIN, TEAG, from Barbados aboard the Industry, master James Porter, bound for Bristol on 8 May 1679. [TNA]

FITZHERBERT, Sir HENRY, arrived in Bridgetown aboard the Renewal in February 1825, from London. [The Barbadian iii]

FITZHERBERT, WILLIAM, was appointed as a Councillor of Barbados in 1770. [PC.Col.V.562]

FITZJAMES, EDWARD, from Barbados, a merchant aboard the Bonadventure, master William Bulkley, bound for London on 24 March 1679. [TNA]

FITZJARRELL, JOHN, from Barbados aboard the Swallow, master Thomas Witlington, bound for Liverpool on 21 May 1679. [TNA]

FITZNICHOLS, MARY, a servant of Richard Michell sr., aboard the Nathaniel, master William Clarke, bound for Boston on 29 April 1679. [TNA]

FITZPATRICK, SARAH ELIZABETH, born 1811, wife of James Evelyn Fitzpatrick, died 20 July 1854, parents of James Evelyn Fitzpatrick, born 1843, died in July 1854. [Christ Church MI]

FITZRANDOLPH, PHILLIP, from Barbados aboard the Unity, master Abraham Wise, bound for 'Saltortudos' on 4 March 1679. [TNA]

FLEAR, FRANCIS, from Barbados aboard the Barbados Merchant, master James Cock, bound for Virginia on 1 October 1679. [TNA]

FLEMING, EDMOND, from Barbados aboard the Society, master Edmond Ditty, bound for Bristol on 4 June 1679. [TNA]

FLETCHER, Brevet Major JOHN WYNNE, born 1785, died 24 October 1824. [St Michael's MI]

FODERINGHAM, HENRY WALCOTT, petitioned for the estate of his brother William Francis Foderingham, a merchant, on 14 October 1825. [The Barbadian iii]

FODERINGHAM, WILLIAM F., died aboard the Servern on passage to England in June 1825. [The Barbadian iii]

FORBES, HENRY, from Barbados, died in Bristol on 24 October 1757. [GM.27.531]

FORBES, WILLIAM, in Barbados, a bond 1 May 1772. [NRS.RD4.248.891]

FORBUSH, JAMES, from Barbados aboard the Two Brothers, master Rice Jefferyes, bound for Jamaica on 13 February 1679. [TNA]

FORBES, FRANCIS, from Barbados aboard the Malaga Merchant, master Roger Hemer, bound for London on 26 July 1679. [TNA]

FORD, FRANCIS, was appointed a Councillor of Barbados in 1767, dead by 1772. [PC.Col.V.562]

FORD, Sir FRANCIS, from Ember, Surrey, died in Barbados on 7 June 1801. [GM.71.859]

FORD, JOHN, a joiner from Wiltshire, an indentured servant bound via Bristol to Barbados in 1660. [BRO]

FORD, WILLIAM, from Barbados, died in Liverpool on 21 June 1802. [GM.72.783]

FORTE, Major NATHANIEL, was appointed Colonel of the St James and St Thomas Militia in September 1825. [The Barbadian iii]

FOSTER, HESTER, from Barbados aboard the Ann and Eliza, master Hugh Reynolds, bound for Liverpool on 14 May 1679. [TNA]

FOSTER, JOHN, a merchant in Barbados in 1660. [CLRO]

FOSTER Reverend REYNOLD, born 1717, Anglican minister of St Philip's from 1747 until his death on 17 February 1749, he had married Anna Marie Holder on 1 February 1749.

FOWLER, JOSHUA, from Barbados aboard the John and Mary, master John Uree, bound for London on 13 May 1679. [TNA]

FOWKE, HENRY, born 1726, a Customs searcher on Barbados, died 17 December 1788, his widow Sarah Fowke, died aged ninety or ninety-six, in November 1825, mother of Thomas Pare Fowke of Barbados and of Henry Fowke late of Tewkesbury, Gloucester. [The Barbadian iii]

FOX, PHILLIS, from Barbados aboard the Mary, master Nicholas Lockwood, bound for Carolina on 29 March 1679. [TNA]

FOX, STEPHEN, from Barbados aboard the Mary, master Nicholas Lockwood, bound for Carolina on 29 March 1679. [TNA]

FRANCO, MOSES, in Bridgetown, 1772. [BDA.Levy]

FRANKLIN, THOMAS, from Barbados aboard the Supply, master Joseph Freeman, bound for London on 26 March 1679. [TNA]

FRANSUM, JOSEPH, from Barbados aboard the barque Blessing, master Francis Watlington, bound for Providence on 31 March 1679. [TNA]

FRAZER, EDMUND, a bachelor in Barbados, Admin., 1649, PCC

FREDERICK, GEORGE MAY DALZELL, born 1831, son of George E. Frederick and his wife Margaret Buchan in Bristol, Archdeacon of Barbados and Rector of St Peter's, Speight Town, died 8 January 1897. [St Peter's, Speight Town, MI]

FREE, JOHN, born 1610, bound from London aboard the Hopewell to Barbados in February 1635. [TNA.E157.20]

FREEMAN, JOSEPH, formerly a corn factor in London, then a merchant in Barbados, died there in April 1808. [GM.78 639]

PEOPLE OF BARBADOS, 1625-1875

FRENCH, LIONEL, in Barbados, probate, 1660, PCC

FRENCH, SAMUEL, from Barbados aboard the ketch Joseph and Mary, master Abraham Knott, bound for New York on 28 May 1679. [TNA]

FRERE, HENRY, was appointed a Councillor of Barbados in 1780. [PC.Col.V.563]

FRERE, JOHN, in Barbados, died in 1759. [GM.29.497]

FRETWELL, RALPH, a merchant in London, bound for Barbados in November 1653. [CLRO.Depoitions.9]

FRITH, SAMUEL, from Barbados aboard the pink Rebecca master Thomas Williams, bound for Virginia on 21 June 1679. [TNA]

FRIZIER, WILLIAM, a gentleman in Barbados, probate, 2 November 1731, [TNA.Prob.11.647.207]

FROIS, JACOB, in Bridgetown, 1772. [BDA.Levy]

FRONTLEROY, JAMES, from Barbados aboard the Prudence and Mary, master Jacob Green, bound for Boston on 23 May 1679. [TNA]

FRYER, WILLIAM, from Whitechapel, died in Barbados, Admin., 1655, PCC

FYERS, JONE, from Barbados aboard the Katherine, master Robert Dapwell, bound for Bristol on 19 March 1679. [TNA]

GAITSKILL, Miss JANE, daughter of Henry Gaitskill in Southwark, London, married Reverend Bryan T. Nurse, in St George's on 15 February 1825. She arrived in Bridgetown aboard the Renewal in February 1825, from London. [The Barbadian iii]

GALE, ROBERT, a merchant in Barbados, an attorney there in November 1659. [CLRO.Deposition.9]

GALL, WILLIAM, born 1674, a carpenter in Barbados, a landowner in 1696. [BDA. Deeds RB3.20.153]

GALLON, JAMES, a tailor in Barbados, 1749, son of John Gallon in Petty, Inverness-shire. [SIL.462]

GAND, RICHARD, born 1616, bound from London aboard the Hopewell to Barbados in February 1635. [TNA.E157.20]

GARCIA, DAVID, in Bridgetown, 1772. [BDA.Levy]

GARDNER, GEORGE, from Barbados aboard the Samaritan, master Valentine Trim, bound for Liverpool on 11 March 1679. [TNA]

GARRETT, WILLIAM, a merchant in Barbados, probate/Admin, 1654, PCC

GARTFORD, WILLIAM, from London, died in Barbados, Admin., 1658, PCC

GASCOINE, JOHN, a merchant in Barbados, 1755. [East Sussex Record Office; Schiffner MSS 2721-7]

GASKIN, JOHN S., of Bushy Park, Barbados, married Mary Matilda Protheroe, third daughter of Thomas S Protheroe of Clifton, in Jersey on 4 June 1844. [GM.ns.23.311]

GASKIN, MARY ELIZABETH, wife of John Sheape Gaskin a Councillor in Barbados, died in London on 18 March 1840. [GM.ns.13.442]

GASKIN, SARAH ELIZA, youngest daughter of Thomas Gaskin, married Edward Gunning, in Barbados, on 24 August 1819. [GM.89.272]

GERISH, BENJAMIN, from Barbados aboard the ketch Mary, master John Gardner, bound for Boston on 22 March 1679. [TNA]

GIBBONS, W B, married Ann Maxwell Hinds Jackman, eldest daughter of John Abel Jackman, and niece of Samuel Hinds a former Speaker of the Barbados Assembly, in Barbados on 5 April 1845. [GM.ns.23.645]

GIBBS, EDWARD, from Barbados aboard the Roebuck, master William Shafto, bound for London on 14 May 1679. [TNA]

GIBBS, ELIZABETH, born 1800, wife of John Gibbs formerly a merchant in Barbados, died in Trinidad on 8 August 1825. [The Barbadian iii]

GIBBS, Sir PHILIP. was appointed a Councillor of Barbados in 1781. [PC.Col.V.563]

GIBBS, RICHARD, from Barbados aboard the Bachelor, master Roger Bagg, bound for Bristol on 6 May 1679. [TNA]

GIBSON, JOSEPH, died in April 1824, 'left a widow and seven children'. [The Barbadian. ii]

GIDEON, ROWLAND, from Barbados aboard the ketch Phoenix, master Robert Flexny, bound for Antigua on 25 October 1679. [TNA]

GIDY, ELIZABETH, born 6 January 1687, died 1 April 1726, wife of Mathew Gidy. [St Lucy's MI]

GILES, J. W., born 1798, died 14 June 1854. [Christ Church MI]

GILL, Mrs MARY, born 2 February 1776, died 14 March 1863. [St Lucy's gravestone]

GILL, WILLIAM, arrived in Bridgetown aboard the Mercy in February 1825. [The Barbadian iii]

GILLBANKS, JOSEPH, Deputy Postmaster General, died in Bridgetown, Barbados, on 24 June 1858. [GM.ns.2/5.313]

GITTENS, JOSHUA MAYERS, son of Judge John Gittens, owner of the Pilgrim plantation in 1816.

GITTENS, JOHN, born 1713, died in February 1768, father of Joshua Gittens. [St Philip's MI]

GITTENS, Mrs MARGARET ANN, born 1 April 1821, died 3 August 1854, mother of Herbert Callender Gittens, born 17 April 1852, died 8 September 1855. [St Philip's MI]

GITTENS, MARTHA ELIZABETH, born 1777, daughter of Benjamin Gittens the Chief Judge of Barbados, died in Bow, Middlesex, on 5 December 1854. [GM.ns.43.110]

GITTES, HENRY, from Barbados aboard the Mary, master Nicholas Lockwood, bound for Carolina on25 April 1679. [TNA]

GLASGOW, Mrs MARY, born 1671, relict of Reverend John Glasgow, died 23 June 1734. [St James, Hole Town, MI]

GODDARD, Reverend ARTHUR, from Barbados, married Miss Barker, daughter of Captain Barker of the Royal Navy, in Bristol on 11 September 1824. [The Barbadian ii]

GODDARD, GILES, in Barbados, Admin., 1652, PCC

GODFRY, GILBERT, a servant of William Bulkley, from Barbados aboard the ketch Neptune, master Joseph Knott, bound for Virginia on 19 August 1679. [TNA]

GODFRY, MARY, from Barbados aboard the Mary, master Nicholas Lockwood, bound for Carolina on 7 April 1679. [TNA]

GODING, JOHN GAY, jr., born 1822, died 18 December 1845. [St Peter's, Speight's Town, MI]

GODMAN, WILLIAM, born 1673, son of Reverend Henry Godman, settled in Barbados as a merchant in 1688, died 1 August 1710. [St Michael's MI]

GODWYN, MORGAN, an Anglican priest in Virginia and Barbados in the 1660s and 1670s, author of 'The Negro's and Indian's Advocate' [London, 1680]

GOGIN, WILLIAM, from Barbados aboard the <u>Bachelor,</u> master Roger Bagg, bound for Bristol on 23 May 1679. [TNA]

GOLDING, PERCIVAL, from Barbados aboard the <u>White Fox,</u> master John Lee, bound for Pool on 18 March 1679; also aboard the <u>Concord,</u> master James Strutt, bound for London on 6 May 1679. [TNA]

GOLDSBURY, VALESIUS SKIPTON, eldest son of Valesius Goldsbury in Longford, Ireland, great grandson of I. A. Goldsbury of Auchnogare, married Isobel Charlotte Perrott, third daughter of Edmund Thomas Perrott in Worcestershire, in Barbados on 8 September 1867. [GM.ns.2/17.647]

GOMEZ, ELIAS, in Bridgetown, 1772. [BDA.Levy]

GOMEZ, ISAAC, with three children, in St Michael's, Barbados, in 1680. [HOT.449]

GOMEZ, RAPHAEL, in Bridgetown, 1772. [BDA.Levy]

GOMEZ, SARAH, in Bridgetown, 1772. [BDA.Levy]

GOODALL, WILLIAM, born 1620 in Hampshire, died 8 November 1690, husband of Jane ...., born 1641, died 19 September 1670. [St Philip's gravestone]

GOODING, JOSEPH, from Barbados aboard the barque <u>Boneta,</u> master Richard Ripley, bound for Jamaica on 12 April 1679. [TNA]

GOODSIR, THO.MAS, born 1827, son of Thomas Goodsir, a Customs Officer in Barbados, died in Greenwich on 9 May 1847. [GM.ns.28.104]

GORDON, EDWARD, born 1728, 'going out to one of the councils in Barbados', accompanied by Miss Mandeville, born 1749, from

London via Portsmouth, aboard the Britannia, bound for Barbados in February 1774. [TNA.T47.9/11]

GORDON, GEORGE, from Barbados aboard the Plantation, master Aser Sharpe, bound for Carolina on 9 August 1679. [TNA]

GORTON, JOHN, a servant of John Brown, from Barbados aboard the ketch Neptune, master Joseph Knott, bound for Virginia on 19 August 1679. [TNA]

GORTON, RICHARD, from Barbados aboard the sloop Rutter, master Edward Duffield, bound for Jamaica on 1 October 1679. [TNA]

GOTHER, HENRY, from Barbados aboard the sloop Rutter, master Edward Duffield, bound for Jamaica on 1 October 1679. [TNA]

GRACE, JANE, aunt of Reverend James F. Neblett, died at an advanced age in February 1825. [The Barbadian iii]

GRAHAM, Captain JAMES, born 1653, died 12 July 1730, father of James Graham, born 1691, died 20 December 1729, his wife Mary, born 1696, died 22 May 1747, their daughter Elizabeth, born 1721, died 16 July 1730. [St Lucy's gravestone]

GRAHAM, ..., son of G Graham of the 21st Fusiliers was born in Barbados on 11 May 1861. [GM.ns.2/11.77]

GRANNUM, RICHARD, born 1768, died 6 October 1820, his wife Amelia Grant, born 1765, died 22 November 1821, parents of Sarah Margaret Grannum, Amelia G. Grannum, Mary Grannum, also William Brian Grannum born 1797, died 13 August 1820 husband of Sarah Elizabeth. [St Thomas MI]

GRANT, WILLIAM H., was appointed Captain Gunner of Ordnance at Pilgrim on 17 May 1825. [The Barbadian iii]

GRASSETT, WILLIAM, a Councillor in Barbados, married Eliza, daughter of J H Barrow on 29 March 1818. [GM.88.368]

GRAY, FANNY, youngest daughter of Dr Gray the Bishop of Bristol, died in Barbados on 20 February 1827. [GM.96.478][St Michael's MI]

GRAY, RICHARD, a citizen and cordiner of London, bound for Barbados, probate, 1655, PCC

GRAY, ROBERT, from Barbados aboard the ketch Endeavour, master Lawrence Colt, bound for New England on 22 July 1679. [TNA]

GRAYFOOT, RACHEL SUSAN, only daughter of John Grayfoot, married Plunkett Standish Lyne Preston a merchant, in Bridgetown, Barbados, on 3 January 1846. [GM.ns.25.421]

GRAYHAM, JAMES, a gentleman in Barbados, probate 29 January 1701, PCC, [[TNA.Prob.11.459.122]

GREAVES, ELIZABETH GRACE, born 18 December 1811, daughter of Thomas W. Greaves and his wife Elizabeth Alice ..., died 16 September 1869, wife of Henry Lawrence. [St Lucy's MI]

GREAVES, FRANCES ANN, born 1794, died 10 September 1823, wife of Charles Whitfoot Greaves. [St Lucy's gravestone]

GREAVES, PERCY LAWRENCE, born 1866, son of Reverend John Lawrence Greaves and his wife Evelina, died 4 October 1876. [St Leonard's MI]

GREAVES, THOMAS W., of Mount Poyer, born 11 June 1792, died 13 June 1823, husband of Elizabeth Alice, who died on 29 May 1817, parents of Edward Austin, born 9 February 1813, died 24 December 1867. [St Lucy's gravestone]

GREEN, RICHARD, from North Piddle, Worcestershire, an indentured servant bound via Bristol for Barbados in December 1658. [BRO]

GREENSLATT, THOMAS, from Barbados aboard the sloop True Friendship, master Charles Callahan, bound for Antigua on 7 October 1679. [TNA]

GREGORIE, R., in Barbados, a letter 7 July 1641, [Buckinghamshire Record Office, Verney pp]

GRESTMICH, JACOBUS, from Barbados aboard the pink Desire, master Thomas Wadham, bound for Pool on 18 March 1679. [TNA]

GRIFFITH, ANN BELL GRANT, fourth daughter of William Griffith a barrister in Barbados, married Michael Angelo of the War Office, in London on 24 April 1862. [GM.ns.2/12.775]

GRIFFITH, LUCY COBHAM, daughter of Thomas Howard Griffith in Barbados, and wife of Dr John Hennen, died in London on 13 September 1845. [GM.ns.24.543]

GRIFFITH, RICHARD SKINNER, born 1807, MD, died 15 October 1833. [St Michael's MI]

GRIFFITH, SARAH, born 1810, died 14 January 1891. [St Michael's MI]

GRIFFITH, THOMAS, born 1732, died 4 August 1795, husband of Jane, born 1737, died 11 July 1796. [St Michael's MI]

GRIFFITHS, WILLIAM, from Cardiganshire, an indentured servant, bound via Liverpool for Barbados in July 1698. [LRO]

GRIFFITH, Sir WILLIAM BRANDFORD, born in Barbados on 11 August 1824, Lieutenant Governor of the Gold Coast from 1879 to 1885, Governor from 1885 to 1895, KCMG, died in Barbados on 18 September 1897. [St Michael's MI]

GRIFFITH, ..., son of William Griffith a Barrister at Law, was born on 11 August 1824. [The Barbadian ii]

GRIFFIN, DENNIS, from Barbados aboard the sloop John and Francis, master John Howard, bound for Antigua on 2 September 1679. [TNA]

GRIFFIN, JOHN, died at Alleynedale of cholera on 27 June 1854. [St Lucy's MI]

GRIGG, ALICE, from Barbados aboard the Mary, master Nicholas Lockwood, bound for Carolina on 10 March 1679. [TNA]

GRIGG, ROBERT, from Barbados aboard the Mary, master Nicholas Lockwood, bound for Carolina on 10 March 1679. [TNA]

GRINFIELD, General WILLIAM, Colonel of the 86th Regiment, born 1744, died 19 November 1803, hisband of Emma Maria Brocas, born 1744, daughter of Reverend John Brocas in Killela, Ireland, died16 November 1803. [St Michael's MI]

GRITLY, ANDREW, a weaver from Taunton, Somerset, an indentured servant, bound via Bristol for Barbados in April 1658. [BRO]

HACKER, FERDINANDO, from Barbados aboard the Fairfax, master Nicholas Fairfax, bound for London on 30 April 1679. [TNA]

HACKETT, ROBERT, from Barbados aboard the Society, master Edmond Ditty, bound for Bristol on 23 May 1679. [TNA]

HALE, BARNABIE, a servant of Colonel Christopher Codrington, from Barbados aboard the barque Dove, master Anthony Jenour, bound for Nevis on 29 October 1679. [TNA]

HALEY, DENNIS, from Barbados aboard the Society, master Edmond Ditty, bound for Bristol on 23 May 1679. [TNA]

HALL, FRANCES J., died 24 September 1838, aged 26 months. [St Thomas MI]

HALL, GILES, jr., from Barbados aboard the ketch John and Mary, master John Perreck, bound for Boston on 31 July 1679. [TNA]

HALL, JOHN, married Miss Tudor in July 1824. [The Barbadian ii]

HALL, MARY, wife of Hugh Hall, daughter of Charles Buckworth, born 1682, died 6 October 1711. [St Michael's MI]

HALL, RICHARD RODERICK, born 1804, died 29 July 1843. [St Thomas gravestone]

HALLET, JOHN, a merchant in Barbados, was appointed an attorney in October 1659. [CLRO.Deposition.9]

HALS, MATHEW, a gentleman in Barbados, died in Gravesend, probate, 18 October 1647, PCC. [TNA.Prob.11.202.77]

HALY, EDWARD B., from Barbados, late in London, died on passage to the West Indies aboard the SS Solway on 7 April 1843. [GM.ns.20.110]

HAMIAS, MOSES, with two children, in St Michael's, Barbados, in 1680. [HOT.449]

HAMILTON, ADAM, from Barbados aboard the ketch William and Susan, master Ralph Parker, bound for New England on 21 March 1679. [TNA]

HAMILTON, CLAUDIUS, in Barbados, probate, 2 April 1713. [TNA.Prob.11 532.290]

HAMILTON, MARY, from Barbados, married William Hemming, a merchant in Dublin on 1 May 1755. [GM.25.236]

HAMILTON, ..., a planter from Tobago, aboard the Three Brothers, from Portsmouth to Barbados in March 1776. [TNA.T47.9/11]

HAMMELL, WILLIAM, died in Barbados on 12 January 1811. [GM.81.395]

HAMPDEN, R DICKSON, a Councillor of Barbados, died there on 8 May 1852. [GM.ns.38.317]

HAMPDEN, SARAH, born 1772, widow of Jarrett Hampden in Barbados, died in Drumlanrig House, Ayr, on 5 February 1848. [GM.ns.29.454]

HAMPSON, WILLIAM, born 1784, eldest son of Edward Hampson in Baldock, Hertfordshire, died in Barbados in June 1807. [GM.77.888]

HANCOCK, ALEXANDER, from Barbados aboard the sloop True Friendship, master Charles Callahan, bound for Antigua on 7 October 1679. [TNA]

HANNEY, GEORGE, Provost Marshal of Barbados, 21 January 1696. [Oxford. Rawl.A241]

HANNINGTON, BERNARD, born 1709, died 14 July 1755. [St Michael's MI]

HANNIS, RICHARD, born 5 November 1667, died 19 May 1752, father of Elizabeth, born 17 January 1729, died 17 August 1733. [St John's MI]

HANBY, RICHARD, born 1612, bound from London aboard the Hopewell to Barbados in February 1635. [TNA.E157.20]

HANNAH, ANDREW, a servant of William Strickland, from Barbados aboard the sloop Katherine, master Andrew Gall, bound for Antigua on 27 November 1679. [TNA]

HANSTEY, JAMES, born 1756, a gentleman from Bath, via Bristol aboard the Eleanor, bound for Barbados in December 1775. [TNA.T47.9/11]

HARBART, LETTIS, a spinster from Bristol, an indentured servant bound via Bristol for Barbados in December 1658. [BRO]

HARBIN, JOHN, a merchant in St Michael's, Barbados, probate, 15 November 1709. [TNA.Prob.11.511.292]

HARBORNE, JOHN, a bachelor, died in Barbados, Admin., 1655, PCC

HARDING, WILLIAM, married Miss Merritt, sister of Richard Merritt, in April 1825. [The Barbadian iii]

HARFIELD, ELINOR, a spinster from Hursley, Hampshire, an indentured servant, bound via Bristol aboard The Dolphin for Barbados in May 1660. [BRO]

HARKER, JOHN, from Barbados aboard the Hope, master John Price, bound for New England on 17 September 1679. [TNA]

HARMSWORTH ROBERT, Clerk of the Markets in Barbados, 21 January 1696. [Oxford, Rawl.A241.122]

HARRIS, EDWARD, from Barbados aboard the Experiment, master Henry Sutton, bound for London on 21 June 1679. [TNA]

HARRIS, JOHN, an indentured servant bound via Bristol for Barbados in December 1658. [BRO]

HARRIS, SARAH, born 1831, youngest daughter of George Cummins the Archdeacon of Trinidad, died in Worthing, Barbados, on 6 March 1853. [GM.ns.39.560]

HARRIS, WARD, born 1712, died 2 June 1761, his wife Elizabeth, born 1721, died 13 January 1791. [St Peter's, Speight's Town, MI]. [St Peter's, Speight's Town, MI]

HARRISON, JOHN, born 1589, bound from London aboard the Hopewell to Barbados in February 1635. [TNA.E157.20]

HARRISON, THOMAS, a mariner in Barbados, probate 9 March 1702, PCC. [TNA.Prob.11.464.43]

HARRISON, THOMAS, born 1689, died 7 June 1746. [St Michael's MI]

HART, WILLIAM, of the Friends Adventure of Barbados, probate, 26 May 1704, PCC. [TNA.Prob.11.476.332]

HARVEY, GRIFFITH, from Barbados aboard the Merchant Bonadventure, master William Bulkley, bound for London on 20 March 1679. [TNA]

HARWOOD, RALPH, born 1612, bound from London aboard the Hopewell to Barbados in February 1635. [TNA.E157.20]

HASELL, PETER, from Barbados aboard the Happy Return, master Isaac Ragg, bound for London on 20 October 1679. [TNA]

HASELL, WILLIAM, from Barbados aboard the Olive Tree, master Thomas Shellan, bound for Bristol on 28 March 1679. [TNA]

HASLER, ..., a planter in Barbados, returned aboard the Three Brothers, from Portsmouth to Barbados in March 1776. [TNA.T47.9/11]

HATTON, ROBERT, from Barbados aboard the Hunter, master Walter Assueros, bound for Surinam on 3 March 1679. [TNA]

HAVILAND, MILES, from Barbados aboard the ketch Swallow, master Joseph Hardy, bound for Rhode Island on 1 April 1679. [TNA]

HAWKSWORTH, WILLIAM, born 1785, died 29 April 1852, husband of Eliza Ann. [St Michael's MI]

HAWTAYNE, GERARD, who died in Barbados, Admin., 1657, PCC

HAWTON, GERARD, from Barbados aboard the Expedition, master John Hardin, bound for London on 1 April 1679. [TNA]

HAYEM, ABRAHAM, from Barbados aboard the James, master William Sweetland, bound for New York on 11 February 1679. [TNA]

HAYES, Captain JOHN, died in Barbados by 1649, husband of Susanne. [CLRO.Deposition.3]

HAYNES, ROBERT JAMES, died on Fraser's Estate, St Joseph, in November 1824. [The Barbadian ii]

HAYNES, ROBERT, jr., of St John, married Miss Reece, daughter of Robert Reece of Christ Church, in September 1825. [The Barbadian iii]

HAYNES, Mrs, wife of Robert Haynes jr, died on Clifton Estate, St John, on 30 July 1824. [The Barbadian ii]

HEALY, WILLIAM, from Barbados aboard the Society, master Edmond Ditty, bound for Bristol on 2 May 1679. [TNA]

HEATH, JOSIAH, married Miss Cheesman in October 1825. [The Barbadian iii]

HEATLY, SAMUEL, of Barbados, now in the parish of Christchurch, London, probate, 1654, PCC

HEBTON, MARGERY, from Barbados aboard the sloop Africa, master Anthony Burgess, bound for the Leeward Islands in 1679. [TNA]

HELMES, JOHN, from Barbados aboard the ketch Nicholas and Rebecca, meeward aster Nicholas Blake, bound for New York on 31 May 1679. [TNA]

HENDERSON, ROBERT, died in Barbados, Admin., 1654, PCC

HENDLY, DANIEL and ELIZA, from Barbados aboard the Olive Tree, master Thomas Sellam, bound for Bristol on 2 April 1679. [TNA]

HENNIGO, ALBRECHT, from Barbados aboard the Judith, master Robert Kingsland, bound for London on 11 March 1679. [TNA]

HERBERT, HENRY, from Barbados aboard the John and Henry, master Thomas Cades, born for Bristol on 14 August 1679. [TNA]

HENRIQUES, RACHEL, in Bridgetown, 1772. [BDA.Levy]

HENRIQUES, SARAH, in Bridgetown, 1772. [BDA.Levy]

HERIOT, Miss, daughter of J Heriot, Deputy Paymaster of the Windward and Leeward Islands, died at White Park, Barbados, in November 1811. [GM.81.658]

HERRICK, ISAAC, from Barbados aboard the ketch William and Susan, master Ralph Parker, bound for New England on 12 March 1679. [TNA]

HETHERINGTON, KATHERINE, from Barbados aboard the pink Greyhound, master Joseph Wasey, bound for London on 9 April 1679. [TNA]

HEWETT, DAVID, a bachelor in Barbados, Admin., 1651, PCC

HEWITT, Mrs MARY JUDITH, born 1788, wife of John Elliott Hewitt, died 9 April 1824. [St Joseph's MI]

HEWITT, WILLIAM, Commissioner for the 'Ceded Islands', and brother of the Lord Chancellor of Ireland, died in Barbados in 1781. [GM.51.489]

HEYES, GEORGE, married Mrs Sarah Howell Massiah, on 8 December 1825. [The Barbadian iii]

HEYWOOD, JOHN, from Barbados aboard the pink ISubmission, master Christopher Newham, bound for London on 24 March 1679. [TNA]

HIGGINSON, JOHN, in St Michael's, Barbados, probate, 13 December 1840. [TNA.Prob.11.1937.326]

HIGGISON, HENRY, from Barbados aboard the Friends Adventure, master John Blades, bound for London on 19 April 1679. [TNA]

HIGLEY, JOHN, from Barbados aboard the ketch Mary, master John Gardner, bound for Boston on 24 March 1679. [TNA]

HILK, JOHN, from Barbados aboard the sloop True Friendship, master Charles Callahan, bound for Antigua on 7 October 1679. [TNA]

HILL, JOHN, born 1616, bound from London aboard the Hopewell to Barbados in February 1635. [TNA.E157.20]

HILL, JOHN, from Barbados aboard the Charles, master Thomas Nash, bound for London on 21 June 1679. [TNA]The Barbadian iii]

HILL, JOHN, married Martha, daughter of John Went on 3 May 1825. [

HILL, JOHN C., born 1789, died 28 March 1838. [St Michael's MI]

HILL, PETER EDWARD, a Captain of the Royal Artillery, married Emily Mary Clarke, second daughter of William Clarke, MD, in Tweedside, Barbados on 26 October 1864. [GM.ns.2/16.108]

HILL, SYON, a merchant of London, bound for Barbados in 1660, a deposition. [CLRO.Deposition.10]

HINCHMAN, THOMAS, a merchant in Barbados, an attorney for Anna Meare, 9 September 1659. [CLRO.Deposition.9]

HINCKS, MATILDA, youngest daughter of Francis Hincks the Governor of the Windward Islands, married Henry Clement Beresford of the 69th Regiment, youngest son of John de la Poer-Beresford, the Colonial Secretary of St Vincent, in Barbados on 23 July 1857. [GM.ns.2/3.456]

HINDS, ELIZABETH, daughter of Benjamin Hinds the Treasurer of Barbados, and wife of John A. Jackman, parents of Ann Maxwell Hinds Jackman who was born 5 April 1825 on Rockless Plantation. [The Barbadian. ii]

HINDS, ..., daughter of Philip L. Hinds, was born in Speightstown on 1 October 1824. [The Barbadian ii]

HINDS, SAMUEL, MD, born 1761, died on Warren's Plantation on 21 July 1824, he married Eleanor Lythcott, daughter of Philip Lythcott the Representative for St James parish, Member of the Council from November 1802, and President from 1821. Samuel Hinds was appointed Attorney General on 21 September 1824. [The Barbadian ii]

HINDS, Reverend WILLIAM, Rector of St Joseph was transferred to St Peter, in place of Reverend Neblett deceased on 8 April 1825. [The Barbadian.iii]; he was appointed Chaplain to the House of Assembly in June 1825. [The Barbadian iii]

HINKSON, JOSEPH, was drowned in Indian River in August 1825. [The Barbadian iii]

HINKSON, Reverend SAMUEL WILLIAM, born 1816, from Farthinghoe, Northamptonshire, died on Colleton Estate, Barbados, in September 1842. [GM.ns.19.102]; petitioned for the states of John Tempro and Amos Tempro, on 17 May 1825. [The Barbadian iii]

HOBBS, ELIZA, from Barbados aboard the <u>Robert,</u> master Richard Cock, bound for London on 20 August 1679. [TNA]

HODGKINSON, ..., daughter of Francis Hodgkinson, was born at Radnor Lodge on 9 January 1825. [The Barbadian iii]

HOLDER, ELIZABETH MURRAY, born 1766, widow of Reverend Henry Holder in Barbados, died in Clifton on 3 April 1848. [GM.ns.29.561]

HOLDESWORTH, ARTHUR, from Barbados aboard the <u>Thomas and Sarah,</u> master James Day, bound for London on 18 September 1679. [TNA]

HOLDIP, HILLIARD, from Barbados aboard the <u>London Merchant,</u> master Edward Desworth, bound for London on 22 April 1679. [TNA]

HOLEMAN, ROGER, from Barbados aboard the sloop <u>True Friendship,</u> master Charles Callahan, bound for Antigua on 24 December 1679. [TNA]

HOLIDAY, MARY, from Barbados aboard the <u>Recovery,</u> master Thomas Chimney, bound for New York on 19 April 1679. [TNA]

HOLLAND, THOMAS, from Barbados aboard the frigate <u>Constant Warwick,</u> Captain Ralph Delavall, bound for London on 3 March 1679. [TNA]

HOLLINGSWORTH, DOWDING, born 1818, son of John and Elizabeth Hollingsworth, died 4 October 1841. [St Lucy's gravestone]

HOLLINGWORTH, THOMAS, born 1774, died in Barbados on 8 March 1815. [GM.ns.85.566]

HOLLINGWORTH, THOMAS, in Barbados, probate, 13 June 1845, PCC. [TNA.Prob.11.2019.247]

HOLLOWAY, RICHARD, from Barbados aboard the sloop <u>Samaritan,</u> master Valentine Trim, bound for Liverpool on 11 March 1679. [TNA]

HOLSEY, RICHARD, from Barbados aboard the sloop <u>Bachelor,</u> master Peter Swaine, bound for the Leeward Islands on 3 May 1679. [TNA]

HOLT, JOSEPH, from Barbados aboard the sloop Hopewell, master Edward Duffield, bound for Jamaica on 6 November 1679. [TNA]

HOLT, ROWLAND, from Barbados aboard the Honour, master Thomas Warren, bound for London on 22 April 1679. [TNA]

HOOK, Colonel HUMPHREY, died 24 March 1668, husband of Joan Hook who died on 22 August 1673. [Cane Garden MI, St Thomas]

HOOK, WILLIAM, from Barbados aboard the barque Hopewell, master Nicholas Morrell, bound for Boston on 2 June 1679. [TNA]

HOOPER, ANTHONY, a merchant bound for Barbados in January 1648. [CLRO.Deposition.2]

HOOPER, DANIEL, from Barbados aboard the ketch Joseph, master Abraham Knott, bound for New York on 17 June 1679. [TNA]

HOOPER, ROBERT, from London, bound for Barbados in 1648, [CLRO.Deposition.2]; settled in Barbados by 1660. [CLRO.Dep.10]; was appointed an attorney in October 1659. [CLRO.Deposition.9]

HOOPER, ROBERT, born 1657, Attorney General of Barbados, died 24 July 1700. [St Michael's MI]

HORNE, GUSTAVUS ADOLPHUS, from Barbados aboard the William and Anne, master Phillip Hanger, bound for London on 3 July 1679. [TNA]

HORONSEN, GARRETT, who died in Barbados, Admin., 1657, PCC

HOUGH, WILLIAM, from Barbados aboard the William and Robert, master Giles Bond, on 21 June 1679. [TNA]

HOW, ELIZA, from Barbados aboard the John's Adventure, master Edward Winslow, bound for Jamaica on 14 June 1679. [TNA]

HOW, THOMAS, a servant of Colonel Christopher Codrington, from Barbados aboard the barque Dove, master Anthony Jenour, bound for Nevis on 29 October 1679. [TNA]

HOWARD, MICHAEL, born 1780, died 29 August 1816, husband of Ann Bell, parents of Michael Skeete Howard and John Robert Howard. [St Peter's, Speight's Town, MI]

HOWE, WILLIAM, in Barbados, a letter from Samuel Pepys recommending ... Skinner, 15 June 1681. [Oxford.Rawl.ms.A183/207]

HOWELL, BENJAMIN C., father of a son born on 1 July 1824 at Eagle Hall. [The Barbadian.ii]; father of a daughter born in November 1825. [The Barbadian iii]

HOWELL, CONRAD ADAMS, born 1767, Treasurer of Barbados, storekeeper, Registrar of Slaves, Colonel of the Militia, and a Vestryman of St Michael's, died at the residence of Philip L. Hinds in Speightstown in August 1824. [The Barbadian ii]

HOWELL, RODERICK ELDER, second son of Thomas Rous Howell, died on 22 March 1825. [The Barbadian iii]

HOWELL, SARAH, from Barbados aboard the barque Providence, master Francis Watlington, bound for Bermuda on 10 April 1679. [TNA]

HOWELL THOMAS J., son of Conrad Howell, was appointed Treasurer and Storekeeper of Barbados, in August 1824. [The Barbadian ii]

HOWELL, ..., daughter of Thomas Rous Howell, was born at Howell Vale, Christ Church, on 18 February 1824. [The Barbadian.ii]

HOWELL, WILLIAM, died in Barbados, Admin., 1654, PCC

HOWLETT, JOHN, a vagrant boy in Bridewell, bound from London on 10 July 1679. for Barbados in 1632.

HUGHS, ANDREW, from Barbados aboard the Amity, , master Benjamin Grore, bound for London on 10 July 1679. [TNA]

HUGHES, J., a sawyer from Merionethshire, an indentured servant bound via Liverpool for Barbados in 1698. [LRO]

HUGHES, RICHARD, from Mould, an indentured servant, bound via Liverpool to Barbados in 1698. [LRO]

HUMBERSTONE, FRANCIS, was commissioned as Captain General and Governor of Barbados, also Vice Admiral Commissary and Deputy on 3 December 1800. [NRS.GD46.7.2]; his letter book 1801 to 1802, [NRS.GD46.7.4]; Letter-books, 1802-1804. [NRS.GD46.7.7]

HUMBLEBY, JOHN, born 1773, died 28 January 1814. [St Michael's MI]; a merchant in Barbados, died on 28 January 1814. [GM.84.408]

HUNCKES, Sergeant Major HENRY, proclaimed Governor of Barbados, 16 March 1639. [Bodleian ms. Bankes.65/37]

HUNT, DENNIS, from Barbados aboard the frigate Coast, master Phillip Varloe, bound for London on 13 June 1679. [TNA]

HUNT, JOHN, from Barbados aboard the Providence, master Timothy Pront, bound for Boston on 28 June 1679. [TNA]

HUNTE, MARY THOMAS, born 1832, died 10 November 1852. [St Philip's MI]

HUNT, WILLIAM, in Barbados, probate 27 February 1719, PCC. [TNA.Prob.11.567.408]

HUNTE, Mrs, died in Bridgetown in July 1824. [The Barbadian. ii]

HURLES, ELIZA, from Barbados aboard the Martin, master Christopher Martin, bound for Newfoundland on 10 April 1679. [TNA]

HURST, WILLIAM, from Barbados aboard the Adventure, master William Johnson, bound for London on 3 May 1679. [TNA]

HUSBAND, RICHARD, Deputy Secretary of Barbados, witness to a deed, dated 1 September 1764. [NRS.RD3224/1.9]

HUTSON, Reverend JOHN, born 1806, Rector of St Andrew's for 25 years, died 18 November 1865, husband of Susanna Jane ...., born 1807, died 12 May 1891. [St Andrew's gravestone]

IFILL, BENJAMIN, born 1775, died 21 September 1835. [St Michael's MI]

IFILL, WILLIAM, MD, born 1803, died in Barbados on 9 March 1855. [GM.ns.43.544]

IMAGE, ..., daughter of J. G. Image, a Captain of the Royal North British Fusiliers, was born in Barbados on 2 December 1863. [GM.ns.2/16.241]

INCE, JOHN, born 1756, died in Barbados on 28 July 1806. [GM.76.875]; was appointed a Councillor of Barbados in 1778. [PC.Col.V.563]

INGLEBY, NICHOLAS, from Barbados aboard the Providence, master Timothy Pront, bound for Boston on 27 June 1679. [TNA]

IRISH, GEORGE, from Barbados aboard the Batchelor, master Roger Bagg, bound for Bristol on 11 June 1679. [TNA]

IRWIN, RICHARD, Governor of Barbados 1720-1721. [Leeds Archives. TN.PO.5A]

ISAAC, THOMAS, a merchant in Barbados, was appointed an attorney in October 1659. [CLRO.Deposition.9]

ISEMONGER, SIMON, from Surrey, aboard the Judith in Barbados, probate, 1656 PCC

ISILL, BENJAMIN, born 1775 in Barbados, died there on 21 September 1835. [GM.ns.4.667]

ISRAELL, DAVID, with five children, in St Michael's, Barbados, in 1680. [HOT.449]

ISRAEL, ISAAC, in Bridgetown, 1772. [BDA.Levy]

ISRAELL, JUDITH, with two children, in St Michael's, Barbados, in 1680. [HOT.450]

IVERY, ELIZABETH, widow of Thomas Ivery a merchant in Barbados, probate, 1653, PCC

JACKMAN, ANN MAXWELL HINDS, born 3 April 1825, daughter of John A. Jackman and his wife Elizabeth daughter of Benjamin Hinds, at Rockless plantation. [Barbadian III]

JACKSON, Lieutenant Colonel CHRISTOPHER, born 1659, died 9 January 1696. [St Michael's MI]

JACKSON, GEORGE, from Barbados aboard the Merchant Bonadventure, master William Bulkley, bound for London on 20 March 1679. [TNA]

JACKSON, JAMES, from Barbados aboard the barque Hopewell, master Thomas Curle, bound for Virginia on 13 August 1679. [TNA]

JACSON, MARY JANE, died on 1 December 1825. [The Barbadian iii]

JACKSON, WILLIAM, from Barbados aboard the Ann and Mary, master John Johnson, bound for Antigua on 14 March 1679. [TNA]

JACOB, JOHN, from Barbados aboard the ketch Providence, master Mark Hunking, bound for New England on 9 April 1679. [TNA]

JAMES, RICHARD, a servant of Colonel Samuel Newton, from Barbados aboard the Joseph, master Stephen Clay, bound for New York on 4 September 1679. [TNA]

JAMES, WILLIAM, from Barbados aboard the Society, master Edmond Ditty, bound for Bristol on 23 May 1679. [TNA]

JARMIN, SYMOUR, from Barbados aboard the sloop Society, master William Guard, bound for Boston on 11 March 1679. [TNA]

JELSON, JOELL, from Barbados aboard the Batchelor master Roger Bagg, bound for Bristol on 11 June 1679. [TNA]

JENKINS, JANE, from Barbados aboard the Lisbon Merchant, master Roger Whitfield, bound for New York on 19 September 1679. [TNA]

70

JENKINS, OWEN, from Barbados aboard the ketch John's Adventure, master Edward Winslow, bound for Jamaica on 17 June 1679. [TNA]

JENNINGS, MICHAEL, from Barbados aboard the ketch Rutter, master Edward Duffield, bound for Jamaica on 26 September 1679. [TNA]

JENNINGS, WILLIAM, from Barbados aboard the sloop True Friendship, master Charles Callahan, bound for Antigua on 7 October 1679. [TNA]

JERRILL, WILLIAM DOWNES, married Georgina Bruce Buchanan, daughter of Captain Colin Buchanan of the 62nd Regiment, and great granddaughter of James Bruce the Chief Judge of Barbados, there on 26 November 1844. [GM.ns.23.420]

JIPSON, SARAH, from Barbados aboard the Mary, master Nicholas Lockwood, bound for Carolina on 29 March 1679. [TNA]

JOHN, MORGAN, from Barbados aboard the barque Dove, master Anthony Jenner, bound for Nevis on 29 October 1679. [TNA]

JOHNSON, JOHN, from Barbados aboard the ketch Joseph, master Abraham Knot, bound for New York on 22 May 1679. [TNA]

JOHNSON, NATHANIEL, from Barbados aboard Friend's Adventure, master John Long, bound for Antigua on 19 April 1679; also, aboard the sloop True Friendship, bound for Antigua on 13 September 1679. [TNA]

JOHNSON, RICHARD, died in Bridgetown in September 1824. [The Barbadian ii]

JOHNSON, THOMAS, who died in Barbados, Admin., 1657, PCC

JOHNSON, THOMAS, died in November 1825, [The Barbadian iii]

JOHNSTONE, ANDREW COCHRANE, in Barbados, a letter, 27 October 1807. [BM. Add.49185]

JOHNSTOUN, Mrs ELIZABETH, born 1660, died 18 July 1729, and her grandson Richard Salter, born 1710, died 6 August 1776. [St George's MI]

JONES, Mrs ABIGAIL, died on 6 September 1824. [The Barbadian ii]

JONES, ALICE, a spinster from Hereford, an indentured servant bound for Barbados in November 1659. [Gloucestershire Record Office. C.10/2]

JONES, BENJAMIN TODD, a Quaker in St Philip, died 1792.

JONES, EDWARD JORDAN, an attorney at law, petitioned for the estate of John Lanahan Jones on 17 May 1825. [The Barbadian iii]

JONES, ELIZA, from Barbados aboard the barque Plantation, master Aser Sharpe, bound for Carolina on 14 August 1679. [TNA]

JONES, HECTOR, from Barbados aboard the sloop Hopewell, master William Murphy, bound for Antigua on 7 November 1679. [TNA]

JONES, JOHN L., a book poster, was accidentally drowned in May 1825. [The Barbadian iii]

JONES, JONES, jr., from Barbados aboard Ann and Eliza, master Hugh Reynolds, bound for Liverpool on 9 May 1679. [TNA]

JONES, MARY, a spinster from Llanlidoll, Montgomeryshire, an indentured servant bound for Barbados in December 1659. [Gloucestershire Record Office.C10.2]

JONES, MILES, from Hereford, an indentured servant, bound via Bristol for Barbados in 1658. [BRO]

JONES, MOSES, from St Bride's, Monmouth, an indentured servant bound via Bristol for Barbados in December 1658. [BRO]

JONES, PETER, from Flintshire, an indentured servant, bound via Liverpool to Barbados in May 1698. [LRO]

JONES, RICHARD, from Carmarthenshire, an indentured servant bound via Bristol for Barbados in December 1658. [BRO]

JONES, RICHARD, from Barbados aboard the Batchelor, master Roger Bagg, bound for Bristol on 22 May 1679. [TNA]

JONES, ROBERT, from Barbados aboard the Rose and Crown, master Thomas Crofts, bound for London on 20 May 1679. [TNA]

JONES, ROWE, a planter in Barbados, returned aboard the Three Brothers, from Portsmouth to Barbados in March 1776. [TNA.T47.9/11]

JONES, SAMUEL, from Barbados aboard the ketch John's Adventure, master Edward Winslow, bound for Jamaica on 18 June 1679. [TNA]

JONES, THOMAS E., born 1803, died in October 1825. [The Barbadian iii]

JONES, WILLIAM, from Barbados aboard the sloop Hopewell, master William Murphy, bound for Antigua on 7 November 1679. [TNA]

JORDAN, ANN, born 1705, died 2 December 1807. [St Michael's MI]

JORDAN, EDWARD, born 1652, died 16 February 1704. [St James, Hole Town, MI]

JORDAN, EDWARD, born 1761, son of Dr Joseph Jordan, died 15 August 1780. [St George's MI]

JOURDAN, JAMES, a debtor in Barbados in 1660, a deposition. [CLRO.Deposition.10]

JORDAN, JAMES, from Barbados aboard the Malaga Merchant, master Roger Horner, bound for London on 13 September 1679. [TNA]

JORDAN, JOSEPH, born 1689, died 29 March 1752, his wife Elizabeth, born 1695, died 6 September 1761. [St George's MI]

JORDAN, JOSEPH, arrived in Bridgetown aboard the Mercy in February 1825. [The Barbadian iii]

JORDAN, WILLIAM, from Barbados aboard the Prudence, master Jacob Green, bound for Boston on 22 May 1679. [TNA]

JORDAN, WILLIAM WALKER, born 1758, died 31 December 1781, brother of above Edward Jordan. [St George's MI]

JORDAN, Miss, eldest daughter of G. W. Jordan, married S. P. Rigaud, HM Astronomer at Richmond, and Professor of Geometry at Oxford, in Barbados on 8 June 1815. [GM.85.562]

JORDAIN, EDWARD, organist, died 28 December 1728. [St Michael's MI]

JOSEPH, EVE, in Bridgetown, 1772. [BDA.Levy]

JOSEPH, JACOB, in Bridgetown, 1772. [BDA.Levy]

JUSTIN, Reverend, and his wife, arrived in Bridgetown aboard the Renewal in February 1825, from London. [The Barbadian iii]

KEANE, MICHAEL, born 1739 in Ireland, settled in St Vincent, died 11 June 1796. [St Michael's MI]

KEELE, THOMAS, a mariner in Barbados, probate, February 1658, PCC

KEELIN, JOSEPH, was appointed a Councillor of Barbados in 1778. [PC.Col.V.563]

KEITH, HENRY, from Barbados aboard the Young William, master Thomas Cornish, bound for Virginia on 2 August 1679. [TNA]

KELLMAN, JAMES C., a Representative for St George in the House of Assembly, died in October 1825. [The Barbadian iii]

KEMBER, DUNSTON, born1615, bound from London aboard the Hopewell to Barbados in February 1635. [TNA.E157.20]

KENNEDY, CHARLES, from Southwark, died in Barbados, Admin., 1652, PCC

KENNEDY, JOHN, and Elinor, his wife, from Barbados aboard the Society, master Edmond Ditty, bound for Bristol on 2 May 1679. [TNA]

KEW, NICHOLAS, from Barbados aboard the barque Resolution, master Thomas Gilbert, bound for Antigua on 29 November 1679. [TNA]

KEYSER, EDMOND, an ironmonger from London, settled in Barbados by October 1659. [CLRO.Deposition.9]

KIELY, Mrs MARY, born in Barbados, emigrated to America in 1822, settled in Hamiltonville and Philadelphia, died on 29 September 1824. [American Daily Advertiser]

KILBEE, WILLIAM, died in Barbados, Admin., 1654, PCC

KILLIKELLY, ELIZABETH, daughter of B. B. Killikelly, died at White River, St Phillip, in April 1824. [The Barbadian.ii]

KING, JANE, a spinster, and an indentured servant, bound via Bristol aboard The Little John for Barbados in March 1660. [BRO]

KING, JOHN HAMPDEN, a barrister and an Assemblyman, married Margaret Hughes Cuppage, only daughter of Adam Cuppage a judge, in Barbados on 30 October 1850. [GM.ns.35.195]

KING, ..., son of Reverend R. F. King, was born on 30 September 1825. [The Barbadian iii]

KING, ROBERT, born 1821, second son of Reverend Robert Francis King of Barbados, a Justice of the Peace and a Magistrate in St George, died in Barbados on 2 July 1859. [GM.ns.2/7.428]

KING, THEOPHILUS, from Nailsworth, Gloucestershire, an indentured servant bound via Bristol for Barbados in December 1658. [BRO]

KING, THOMAS, born 1662, died 11 November 1722. [St James, Hole Town, MI]

KING, WILLIAM, from Barbados aboard the Friend's Adventure, master Edward Blades, bound for London on 24 April 1679. [TNA]

KIRTON, FRANCIS, died in Bridgetown in May 1824. [The Barbadian.ii]

KIRTON, JOHN, MD, died 15 July 1738, his wife Ann, born 1700, died 1 August 1765. [Christ Church MI]

KNAPTON, THOMAS, from New Sarum, Wiltshire, died in Barbados, Admin., 1658, PCC

KOPLEE, JACOB, born 1666, died 26 August 1722. [St Michael's MI]

KYTE, JOHN, from Barbados aboard the Prudence and Mary, master Jacob Green, bound for Boston on 28 May 1679. [TNA]

LADSON, JOHN, from Barbados aboard the barque Plantation, master Aser Sharpe, bound for Carolina on 13 August 1679. [TNA]

LANE, MARGERY, an indentured servant, bound via Bristol for Barbados in 1658. [BRO]

LANGDON, JOHN, sr., who died in Barbados, Admin., 1657, PCC

LANGFORD, HARRY, from Barbados aboard the Joseph, master Stephen Clay, bound for New York on 2 September 1679. [TNA]

LANGLEY, WILLIAM, from Barbados aboard the Brothers Adventure, master John Sellock, bound for New York on 16 April 1679. [TNA]

LANGTON, THOMAS, from Barbados aboard the ketch Prosperous, master David Fogg, bound for Virginia on 12 May 1679. [TNA]

LARGE, VINCENT, died in Barbados, Admin., 1652, PCC

LARDNER, MARIAN, only daughter of J Lardner in Barbados, married Lieutenant R H Vetch of the Royal Engineers, in Dominica on 29 July 1863. [GM.ns.2/15.498]

LASCELLES, Miss, niece of Admiral Holbourne, married Godney Clarke jr, in Barbados on 15 October 1762. [GM.32.503]

LATTER, JOHN, died in Barbados, Admin., 1649, PCC

LAURENCE, THOMAS, a husband from Gloucester, an indentured servant bound for Barbados in November 1659. [Gloucestershire Record Office. C.10/2]

LAURIE, HENRY, Commander of the <u>Surat Castle of Barbados</u>, probate, 1 September 1798, PCC. [TNA.11.1312.79]

LAVINE, ISAAC, in Barbados, died in April 1764. [GM.34.250]

LAW, CHRISTIAN ANN, wife of George Law, died on 8 August 1825. [The Barbadian iii]

LAW, GEORGE, in Barbados, accepted a bill of exchange drawn of a Glasgow merchant on 27 April 1751, see protest. [NRS.RD2.170.187]

LAW, JOSEPH, born 1800, son of Joseph Law in Barbados, died in London on 19 November 1816, and was buried in St Michael's, Cornhill. [GM.86.478]

LAW, THOMAS, a husbandman from Barnwood, Gloucestershire, an indentured servant bound for Barbados in December 1659. [Gloucestershire Record Office.C10.2]

LAWRENCE, JOHN HENRY, born 1812, a master mariner, died 9 July 1852. [St Michael's MI]

LAWRENCE, MARY, born 1791, wife of John Lawrence late Assistant Commissary General, died at St Ann's on 19 October 1824. [The Barbadian ii]

LAWRENCE, Reverend, arrived in Bridgetown aboard the <u>Concord</u> from Bristol in February 1825. [The Barbadian iii]

LAWSON, SOPHIA DELAFOSSE, born 1836, daughter of C Lawson the Archdeacon of Barbados, died in St James, Barbados, on 26 May1859. [GM.ns.2/9.197]

LAWTON, JOHN, married Miss Edwards in October 1825. [The Barbadian iii]

LEACOCK, HENRIETTA MALTBY, daughter of Joseph Leacock at Mount Servitor, Barbados, died in Lee, Kent, on 12 July 1820. [GM.90.93]

LEACOCK, JOHN WRONG, born 1772, died 26 March 1850, husband of Rebecca Townsend, born 1769, died 1 November 1831. [St Lucy's MI]

LEACOCK, SAMUEL, born 1764, died 19 October 1828. [St Lucy's gravestone]

LEACOCK, ..., daughter of John H. Leacock MD, was born in November 1824. [The Barbadian ii]

LEADER, RICHARD, a merchant in Barbados in 1657. [CLRO. Deposition, 1 October 1660].

LEAK, JOHN, a merchant in Barbados, attorney for John Godscall a merchant in London, a deposition in 1658. [CLRO.M8]

LEALTAD, Mrs HANNAH, died 1803. [Bridgetown gravestone]

LEE, HENRY, from Barbados aboard the ketch Unity, master James Rainy, bound for Virginia on 1 April 1679. [TNA]

LEE, HENRY, from Barbados aboard the Martin, master Christopher Martin, bound for Newfoundland on 3 April 1679; from Barbados aboard the Happy Returns, master Isaac Rand, bound for London on 25 October 1679. [TNA]

LEE, RICHARD, from Barbados aboard the pink Rebecca, master Thomas Williams, bound for Virginia   on 17 July 1679. [TNA]

LEE, THOMAS, arrived in Barbados from London aboard the Frances from Liverpool in July 1824. [The Barbadian.ii]

LEITH, Sir JAMES, Governor of Barbados, died in Pilgrim, Barbados, on 16 October 1816. [GM.86.566]

LE ROUX, JACOB, from Barbados aboard the ketch Dove, master John Grafton, bound for Antigua on 29 July 1679. [TNA]

LESLIE, Mrs KATHARINE C., died on 20 August 1824. [The Barbadian ii]

LEWGAR, JOHN, from Barbados aboard the Friendship, master John Williams, bound for London on 8 August 1679. [TNA]

LEWIS, Reverend JOHN GLASGOW, BA of Pembroke College, Oxford, was installed as Rector of St Andrew's on 14 July 1825. [The Barbadian iii]

LEWIS, MORGAN, and his wife Katherine, indentured servants bound via Bristol to Barbados or the Leeward Islands in December 1660. [BRO]

LEWIS, OLIVER, an indentured servant from Ludlow, Shropshire, bound from Bristol for 4 years in Barbados, in September 1658. [BRO]

LEWIS, THOMAS, born 1789 in Devon, second son of Admiral Sir Thomas Louis, a merchant in Barbados from 1813, died 9 February 1862. [St Michael's MI]

LEWIS, Reverend, arrived in Bridgetown aboard the Concord from Bristol in February 1825. [The Barbadian iii]

LEWSBY, JOHN, from Poplar, Stepney, died at sea bound for Barbados, probate. 1655, PCC

LIBBY, Captain, of the sloop Thomas Spencer, married Miss Whitehouse on 31 July 1824. [The Barbadian ii]

LICORISH, JOHN, churchwarden of St Andrew's church in June 1825. [The Barbadian iii]

LILBURNE, RICHARD, from Barbados aboard the ketch Mary and Sarah, master George Conway, bound for Providence on 24 November 1679. [TNA]

LILLINGTON, MARGARET, wife of Captain George Lillington, who died on 3 June 1680. [Cane Garden MI, St Thomas]

LIMNER, WILLIAM, a planter at St Peter on the Mount, Barbados, probate, 1654, PCC

LINDO, ABRAHAM, jr., in Bridgetown, 1772. [BDA.Levy]

LINDO, ISAAC, in Bridgetown, 1772. [BDA.Levy]

LINDO, JACOB, youngest son of David Lindo, died in July 1824. [The Barbadian ii]

LLOYD, JOHN, from Barbados aboard the Barbados Merchant, bound for the Leeward Islands on 28 August 1679. [TNA]

LOCK, ANN, from Barbados aboard the ketch William and Susan, master Ralph Parker, bound for New England on 18 March 1679. [TNA]

LOINSWORTH, AUGUSTE PAINTING, in Barbados, eldest son of A L Loinsworth MD, married Augusta Titt, youngest daughter of Thomas Titt of Brighton, in London on 23 June 1851. [GM.ns.36.315]

LONGSON, WILLIAM, from Barbados aboard the ketch John's Adventure, master Edward Winslow, bound for Jamaica on 17 June 1679. [TNA]

LONSDALE family, planters in Barbados, papers 1670-1737. [Cumberland Record Office]

LOPES, ABRAHAM, from Barbados aboard the Hope, master Joseph Ball, bound for London on 21 April 1679. [TNA]

LOPES, ABRAHAM, with two children, in St Michael's, Barbados, in 1680. [HOT.449]

LOPEZ, ELIAH, with five children, in St Michael's, Barbados, in 1680. [HOT.449]

LOPES, MATTHIAS, in Bridgetown, 1772. [BDA.Levy]

LOPEZ, RACHELL, with four children, in St Michael's, Barbados, in 1680. [HOT.450]

LOPEZ, TELLES ABRAHAM, from Barbados aboard the Recovery, master James Browne, bound for Jamaica on 31 December 1679. [TNA]

LORAINE, HENRY JAMES, born 1801, son of Sir William Loraine of Kirkharle, Northumberland, an Ensign of the 4th Regiment, died 23 December 1821. [St Michael's MI]

LORD, GABRIEL, died in 1803. [St James, Hole Town MI]

LORD, Mr, arrived in Barbados from London aboard the Frances from Liverpool in July 1824. [The Barbadian.ii]

LOUIS, THOMAS, born in Devon in 1789, a merchant in Barbados, died 9 February 1862. [St Michael's MI]

LOUZADA, AARON BARUH, born 1703, died 24 March 1768, his wife Ester Sarah, born 1708, died 20 October 1744. [Bridgetown gravestone]

LOUSADA, EMMANUEL BARUCH, in Bridgetown, 1772. [BDA.Levy]

LOVELL, WILLIAM, from Wedmore, Somerset, an indentured servant bound via Bristol for Barbados in December 1658. [BRO]

LOWE, JOSEPH, died 31 May 1827, buried in St Andrew's churchyard. [St Michael's MI]

LOWE, Dr and Miss Lowe, arrived in Bridgetown aboard the Concord from Bristol in February 1825. [The Barbadian iii]

LOWTHER, CHRISTOPHER, a servant of Colonel Henry Drax, from Barbados aboard the Honour, master Thomas Warren, bound for London on 22 April 1679. [TNA]

LUCAS, Mrs MARY, born 1755, died in November 1825, wife of Nathan Lucas. [The Barbadian iii]

LUNAH, Mrs, wife of Phineas Nunes, died in Swan Street, Bridgetown, on 1 February 1825. [The Barbadian iii]

LYDIATT, TIMOTHY, from Barbados aboard the William and John, master Samuel Legg, bound for Boston on 28 May 1679. [TNA]

LYLE, JOHN, Speaker of the Assembly of Barbados, died on 27 May 1767. [GM.37.382]

LYNCH, HARRIET, petitioned for the estate of Eleanor Lynch on 8 November 1825. [The Barbadian iii]

LYNCH, MORGAN, a servant of John Codrington, from Barbados aboard the barque Resolution, master Thomas Gilbert, bound for Antigua on 29 November 1679. [TNA]

LYNCH, NICHOLAS, with his wife Alice from Barbados aboard the barque Adventure, master Christopher Berron, bound for Antigua on 17 February 1679. [TNA]

LYNCH, PATRICK J. D., petitioned for the estate of Sarah Eleanor Lynch deceased, left unadministered by Dominick Lynch, in April 1825. [The Barbadian iii]

LYNCH, RICHARD, from Barbados aboard the sloop True Friendship, master Charles Callahan, bound for Nevis on 16 September 1679. [TNA]

LYNCH, SAMUEL SMITH, a Lieutenant of the 1st West Indies Regiment of Barbados, married Catherine Rebecca Cox, in Demerara in February 1824. [The Barbadian.ii]

LYNE, CHRISTOPHER, from Barbados aboard the   Recovery, master James Browne, bound for Jamaica on 22 December 1679. [TNA]

LYNN, ROBERT, from Barbados aboard the Malaga Merchant, master Roger Homer, bound for London on 13 September 1679. [TNA]

LYON, MATTHIAS, in Bridgetown, 1772. [BDA.Levy]

LYTCOT, LEONARD, from Barbados aboard the Supply, master Joseph Freeman, bound for London on 26 March 1679. [TNA]

LYTCOTT, NICHOLAS, died in Barbados around 1647. [CLRO.Deposition.2]

LYTE, Colonel PAUL, died in 1687, father of Colonel Paul Lyte, died 1708, his wife Jane Jones, born 1683, died 13 October 1755, and their son John Lyte. [St George's MI]

MABBOTT, RICHARD, an indentured servant bound via Bristol for Barbados in December 1660. [BRO]

MACALPIN, JOHN PILGRIM, infant son of Thomas MacAlpin, died in October 1825. [The Barbadian iii]

MACBREEDY, JOHN KING, born 1789, Assistant Commissary General, died 12 May 1843. [St Paul's MI]

MCCLURE, SAMUEL RICHARD, infant son of Samuel McClure, died in December 1824. [The Barbadian ii]

MACDANIEL, PATRICK, from Barbados aboard the ketch Neptune, master Joseph Knott, bound for Virginia on 13 August 1679. [TNA]

MACKAY, ..., a tavern-keeper on the wharf of Barbados in 1749. [SIL.462]

MCKENZIE, THOMAS, from Barbados, died in Dunkirk in 1831. [GM.101.652]

MACCLAHAN, OWEN, from Barbados aboard the Society, master Edmond Ditty, bound for Bristol on 30 May 1679. [TNA]

MACCUEREE, JOHN, from Barbados aboard the pink Rebecca, master Thomas Williams, bound for Virginia on 10 July 1679. [TNA]

MACMASH, CHARLES, from Barbados aboard the Roebuck, master William Shafto, bound for London on 8 May 1679. [TNA]

MCNEAL, THEOPHILIUS, from Barbados, died on 18 September 1776. [GM.46.436]

MACKAY, ..., daughter of Commissary General Mackay, was born in October 1824. [The Barbadian ii]

MADDRIN, ANN, a widow, died in Barbados, Admin., 1655, PCC

MADDOX, JONE, from Barbados aboard the ketch Beginning, master William Play, bound for New York on 19 March 1679. [TNA]

MADEN, PATRICK, from Barbados aboard the sloop True Friendship, master Charles Callahan, bound for Antigua on 1 October 1679. [TNA]

MAGWAINE, OWEN, from Barbados aboard the Industry, master James Porter, bound for Bristol on 14 May 1679. [TNA]

MAHANE, JOHN, from Barbados aboard the Industry, master James Porter, bound for Bristol on 24 May 1679. [TNA]

MAHANE, JOSEPH, a servant of Henry Quintyne, from Barbados aboard the barque Plantation, master Aser Sharpe, bound for Carolina on 12 August 1679. [TNA]

MAHONY, DANIEL, from Barbados aboard the Friends Adventure, master John Long, bound for Antigua on 28 April 1679. [TNA]

MAJOR, WILLIAM, from Barbados aboard the barque Blessing, master Francis Watlington, bound for Providence on 17 April 1679. [TNA]

MALTBY, RICHARD, a merchant, died in Barbados on 12 September 1816. [GM.86.465]

MANERICK, NATHANIEL, from Barbados aboard the ketch Phoenix, master Robert Flexny, bound for Antigua on 21 October 1679. [TNA]

MANNEN, ANDREWS, from Barbados aboard the Mary, master Nicholas Lockwood, bound for Carolina on 8 April 1679. [TNA]

MANNING, REBECCA FARRELL, widow of Joseph Carter Manning, petitioned for Letters of Guardianship to the person and estate of her son Thomas Davis Manning, on 3 September 1824. [The Barbadian ii]

MANNING, T. J., of Barbados, married Ann Catherine Rose Nassau, daughter of Frederick Nassau of St Osyth Priory, Essex, in Kendal on 15 August 1825. [GM.95.270]

MANSELL, ROBERT, from Barbados aboard the Richard and Mary, master Samuel Fitch, bound for New England on 21 July 1679. [TNA]

MARRIOTT, ROBERT, in Barbados, was appointed an attorney on 23 November 1659. [CLRO.Deposition.9]

MARRIOTT, ROBERT, from Barbados aboard the Recovery, master James Browne, bound for Jamaica on 23 December 1679. [TNA]

MARROW, CORNELIUS and KATHERINE, from Barbados aboard the Society, master Edmond Ditty, bound for Bristol on 23 May 1679. [TNA]

MARSH, THOMAS, with MARY and SUSAN, from Barbados aboard the Society, master Edmond Ditty, bound for Bristol on 11 June 1679. [TNA]

MARSHALL, JAMES, born 1750. A merchant in London, with his wife, born 1752, from London aboard the Marshall, bound for Barbados in April 1774. [TNA.T47.9/11]

MARSHALL, JARVIS, from Barbados aboard the James, master James Sweetland, bound for New York on 28 January 1679. [TNA]

MARSHALL, Mrs MARTHA J., died in Bridgetown in July 1824. [The Barbadian ii]

MARSHALL, ROBERT, in Barbados, probate, 9 January 1640, [TNA.Prob.11.82.20]

MARSHALL, WILLIAM, born 1805, died 14 February 1820. [St Thomas gravestone]

MARTIN, NICHOLAS, a merchant in Barbados, an attorney in 1658. [CLRO.Dep.10]

MASON, SYLAM, from Barbados aboard the William and John, master Samuel Legg, bound for Boston on 19 May 1679. [TNA]

MASSEY, WILLIAM, died in Barbados, Admin. 1660, PCC

MASSIAH, ABRAHAM, in Bridgetown, 1772. [BDA.Levy]

MASSIAH, ANGEL, in Bridgetown, 1772. [BDA.Levy]

MASSIAH, BENJAMIN, in Bridgetown, 1772. [BDA.Levy]

MASSIAH, HESTER, in Bridgetown, 1772. [BDA.Levy]

MASSIAH, ISAAS DE PIZA, born 1763, died in November 1824. [Bridgetown gravestone], [BDA.171.535.38] [The Barbadian ii]

MASSIAH, MORDECAI, in Bridgetown, 1772. [BDA.Levy]

MASSIAH, MORDECAI BURGES, born 1767, died 31 May 1801. [Bridgetown gravestone]

MASSIAH, SIMEON, in Bridgetown, 1772. [BDA.Levy]

MASTERS, JOSEPH, from Barbados aboard the Patience, master Thomas Hudson, bound for London on 11 February 1679. [TNA]

MASTERS, MARTHA, from Barbados aboard the Patience, master Thomas Hudson, bound for London on 11 February 1679. [TNA]

MATHEWS, Captain FREDERICK, son of Colonel Mathews of Chelsea College, a magistrate, died in Barbados on 15 September 1836. [GM.ns.6.668]

MATTHEW, GEORGE, from Barbados aboard the Hannah and Eliza, master Richard Pix, bound for London on 17 May 1679. [TNA]

MATTHEWS, GEORGE, from Barbados aboard the pink Eliza, master John Bonnel, bound for Boston on 16 July 1679. [TNA]

MATTHEWS, JOHN, a mariner bound for Barbados, probate, 23 July 1740, PCC. [TNA.Prob.11.704.121]

MATTHEW, PETER, from Denbighshire, an indentured servant bound via Liverpool for Barbados in 1698. [LRO]

MATTSON, BENJAMIN, from Barbados aboard the John and Mary, master Edward Calcutt, bound for London on 7 April 1679. [TNA]

MATTSON, MATTHEW, from Barbados aboard the Concord, master William Foster, bound for London on 18 June 1679. [TNA]

MAULE, THOMAS, from Barbados aboard the ketch <u>William and John,</u> master John Saunders, bound for New England on 10 April 1679. [TNA]

MAVERICK, ELIZABETH MARY, daughter of Samuel Maverick and wife of Anthony Gregg MD, died 23 October 1790. [St Andrew's gravestone]

MAWFAS, RICHARD, a merchant in Barbados, in London in June 1657. [CLRO.Deposition.9]

MAXWELL, JAMES, a merchant in St Michael's, Barbados, probate 11 March 1814, PCC. [Prob.11.1554.111]

MAXWELL, Miss, married Henry Beckels, in Barbados on 28 September 1762. [GM.32.503]

MAY, JAMES, died at sea when bound for Barbados, probate, 1655, PCC

MAYCOCK, DOTTIN, born 1742, MA, Solicitor General of Barbados, died 11 July 1793, husband of Catharine, born 1764, died 14 February 1849. [St Michael's MI]

MAYCOCK, JAMES DOTTIN, infant son of Reverend Dottin Maycock, died on 26 March 1825. [The Barbadian iii]

MAYERS, BENJAMIN, born 1764, a former Assemblyman, died in Tenby, Barbados, on 3 June 1854. [GM.ns.42.201]

MAYERS, JAMES BENJAMIN, born 1792, died 13 October 1854, husband of Dorothy ....., born 1794, died 18 November 1853. [St Joseph's MI]

MAYNARD, GEORGE, Chief Justice of the Court of Common Plea in Barbados, died there on 30 May 1818. [GM.88.373]

MAYNARD, JAMES, a servant of Matthew Williams, from Barbados aboard the <u>Old Head of Kingsale,</u> master Robert Barker, bound for London on 4 January 1679. [TNA]

MAYNARD, JOHN, a merchant in Barbados, probate, 23 February 1649, PCC. [TNA.Prob.11.207.288]

MAYNARD, JONAS, born 1695, died 3 August 1781, husband of Christian Mercy Maynard, his fourth wife, born 1725, died 23 March 1777. [St Michael's MI]

MEDINAH, LEAH, with seven children, in St Michael's, Barbados, in 1680. [HOT.449]

MEELL, JANE, born 1661, died 23 July 1680, wife of Thomas Meell a surgeon, parents of John Meell, born 1676, died in July 1778. [St George's MI]

MEFFIAT, SIMON, a merchant in Barbados, married Deborah Bilenfaite, in 1768. [GM.38.198]

MELLOBY, JAMES, from Barbados aboard the Virgin, master Thomas Allamby, bound for Virginia on 4 October 1679. [TNA]

MELONY, TIMOTHY, from Barbados aboard the Ann and Mary, master John Johnson, bound for Antigua on 14 March 1679. [TNA]

MENDEZ, ISAAC, born 1675, son of Joseph Mendez, died 30 December 1696. [Bridgetown gravestone]

MENDS, WILLIAM FISHER, Deputy Commissary General, married Mary Vardon Jackson, eldest daughter of the Reverend W. W. Jackson a military chaplain, in Barbados on 16 February 1860. [GM.ns.2/8.506]

MENVILLE, PETER J, born 1795, a merchant in Barbados from there to Newport, USA, aboard the Indian Hunter of New York, master John Brown, in 1820.

MERCADO, MOSES, with five children, in St Michael's, Barbados, in 1680. [HOT.449]

MERRICKE, KATHERINE, a spinster from Abbeydore, Herefordshire, an indentured servant bound for Barbados in December 1659. [Gloucestershire Record Office.C10.2]

MERRING, Lieutenant Colonel JOHN, born 1661, died 28 August 1710. [St Michael's MI]

MERRITT, WILLIAM JOHN, born 1825, second son of Reverend Richard Robinson Merritt, St Michael's, Barbados, died 11 June 1842. [GM.ns.18.335]

MERTON, RICHARD, from Denbighshire, an indentured servant bound via Liverpool for Barbados in 1698. [LRO]

MEZA, ISACK, with three children, in St Michael's, Barbados, in 1680. [HOT.450]

MICHELL, JOHN, from Barbados aboard the Nathaniel, master William Clarke, bound for Boston on 25 April 1679. [TNA]

MICHELL, RICHARD, from Barbados aboard the Nathaniel, master William Clarke, bound for Boston on 25 April 1679. [TNA]

MIDDLETON, ARTHUR, from Barbados aboard the barque Plantation, master Aser Sharpe, bound for Carolina on 14 August 1679. [TNA]

MIDDLETON, HENRY, who died in Barbados, Admin., 1657, PCC

MILES, JOHN, a yeoman and an indentured servant, bound via Bristol aboard The Little John for Barbados in March 1660. [BRO]

MILLER, S., MD, born 1779, formerly a physician in Barbados, died in Chelmsford on 15 May 1860. [GM.ns.2/9.106]

MOE, IRENAEUS, was appointed a Councillor of Barbados in 1768. [PC.Col.V.562]

MONTAGUE, RALPH, a merchant from Bristol, died in Lewis's Hotel, Bridgetown, Barbados on 24 February 1824, and was buried in St Michael's church on 24 February 1824. [GM.94.647][The Barbadian.ii]

MOORE, Mrs DOROTHY, born 1787, daughter of Cholmeley Willoughby, wife of Edward Henry Moore, died 6 July 1819, mother of Francis Henry Moore, born 1806, died 15 November 1816. [St Michael's MI]

MOORE, WILLIAM, Deputy Surveyor and Auditor of Barbados in 1757. [NRS.GD45.17.1]

MOORE, WILLIAM C., jr., born 1789, died on 26 January 1825. [The Barbadian iii]

MOORE, ..., daughter of Henry Moore, was born at Welch cottage in November 1824. [The Barbadian ii]

MORECOCK, THOMAS, from Barbados aboard the Happy Return, master Isaac Baird, bound for London on 25 October 1679. [TNA]

MORENO, AARON, in Bridgetown, 1772. [BDA.Levy]

MOREWOOD, ANTHONY, a bachelor of Barbados, Admin., 1652, PCC

MORGAN, EDWARD, from Barbados aboard the Society, master Edmond Ditty, bound for Bristol on 24 May 1679. [TNA]

MORGAN, JAMES, born 1828, a surgeon, eldest son of Reverend Allen Morgan in Nant-y-Derry, Monmouthshire, died in Barbados on 31 March 1853. [GM.ns.40.97]

MORGAN, JOHN, in Barbados, probate, 31 December 1663, [TNA.Prob.11.312.560]

MORGAN, JOHN, from Barbados aboard the Society, master Edmond Ditty, bound for Bristol 8 May 1679. [TNA]

MORGAN, MILLICENT, born 1746, wife of Septun Morgan, died 9 September 1768. [St James, Hole Town, MI]

MORGAN, THOMAS, from Barbados aboard the Batchelor, master Roger Bagg, bound for Bristol on 14 May 1679. [TNA]

MORRELL, NICHOLAS, from Barbados aboard the Prudence and Mary, master Jacob Green, bound for Boston on 28 May 1679. [TNA]

MORRIS, HOWELL, in Gravesend, trading with Barbados, probate, 1654, PCC

MORRIS, ISAAC, from Barbados aboard the ketch Beginning, master William Play, bound for New York on 18 March 1679. [TNA]

MORRIS, MARY, born 14 March 1694, daughter of Major Robert Morris and wife of James Do...n, died 12 July 1713. [St Andrew's gravestone]

MORRIS, THOMAS, a yeoman from Carmarthen, an indentured servant bound via Bristol to Barbados in 1660. [BRO]

MORRIS, RICHARD, from London, died in Barbados, Admin., 1654, PCC

MORRIS, WILLIAM, from Barbados aboard the Society, master William Guard, bound for Boston on 10 March 1679. [TNA]

MOSELY, RICHARD, from Barbados aboard the William and John, master Samuel Legg, bound for Boston on 24 May 1679. [TNA]

MOUNTACK, ANDREW, from Barbados aboard the Eliza, master Alexander Mattison, bound for Holland on 16 September 1679. [TNA]

MOUNTAINE, JOHN, from Barbados aboard the sloop True Friendship, master Charles Callahan, bound for Antigua on 7 October 1679. [TNA]

MUNDY, EDWARD MILLER, born 1800, son of Edward Miller Mundy of Shipley Hall, Derby, died in Barbados on 29 January 1849. [GM.ns.32.96]

MURPHY, DANIEL, from Barbados aboard the Industry, master James Porter, bound for Bristol on 13 May 1679. [TNA]

MURRAY ELIZABETH, second daughter of William Murray in Barbados, married Lieutenant Colonel S H Berkley of the 16th Regiment, in Barbados on 24 February 1818. [GM.88.464]

MUSKETT, WILLIAM, from Barbados aboard the sloop Rutter, master Edward Duffield, bound for Jamaica on 2 October 1679. [TNA]

MUSSON, ..., daughter of S J Musson in Barbados, was born in Upper Norwood on 1 December 1867. [GM.ns.3/5.101]

MUTER, AGNES, born 1823, daughter of Robert Muter a Lieutenant Colonel of the Royal Canadian Rifles, wife of H Stanley Jones, died in Barbados on 22 May 1854. [GM.ns.42.201]

MYERS, Lieutenant General Sir WILLIAM, born 1752, Commander of H.M. Forces on Barbados, died 29 July 1805. [St Michael's MI]

NAMIAS, DAVID, with nine children, in St Michael's, Barbados, in 1680. [HOT.450]

NASH, JOHN, in Barbados, attorney for Philip Wingfield a baker in London, in 1658. [CLRO.Deposition9]

NASH, RICHARD, an indentured servant, bound via Bristol for Barbados in 1658. [BRO]

NASH, WILLIAM, of St Michael's parish, petitioned the Privy Council Colonial on 27 March 1767. [Acts PCCol.V.55]

NASY, DANIEL, from Barbados aboard the Hope, master John Price, bound for New England on 18 September 1679. [TNA]

NAUARO, ARON, with seven children, in St Michael's, Barbados, in 1680. [HOT.449]

NAUARO, JUDITH, with two children, in St Michael's, Barbados, in 1680. [HOT.450]

NAUARRO, SAMUEL, with four children, in St Michael's, Barbados, in 1680. [HOT.450]

NEAGLE, MARTIN, from Barbados aboard the Young William, master Thomas Cornish, bound for Virginia on 4 August 1679. [TNA]

NEBLETT, Mrs, wife of Reverend James F. Neblett, died at St Peter's Parsonage on 15 January 1824. [The Barbadian.ii]

NEBLETT, Miss, daughter of Reverend James F. Neblett, died on 4 May 1824. [The Barbadian.ii]

NEEDLER, JOHN, from Barbados aboard the pink Rebecca master Thomas Williams, bound for Virginia on 22 July 1679. [TNA]

NEVILL, JOHN, from Barbados aboard the Society, master William Guard, bound for Boston on 7 March 1679. [TNA]

NEVILL, JOHN, from Barbados aboard the Pearl, master Edward Pevison, bound for the Leeward Islands on 4 September 1679. [TNA]

NEVILLE, ..., from Barbados, died in London on 22 November 1777. [GM.48.551]

NEWTON, ABIGAIL, from Barbados aboard the Eliza, master John Bonner, bound for Boston on 15 July 1679. [TNA]

NICHOLLS, JOHN FRANK, born 1764, died 16 December 1807. [St Michael's MI]

NICKS, JOHN, born 1612, bound from London aboard the Hopewell to Barbados in February 1635. [TNA.E157.20]

NIGHTINGALE family in Barbados papers, 1654-1680. [Essex Record Office. D/DRg1/148-158]

NILES, CHARLES PHILLIPS, married Sarah Gittens Sparrock on 18 July 1825. [The Barbadian iii]

NOAKE, Mrs MARGARET, wife of Richard Noake, died 28 July 1677. [St Philip gravestone]

NOELL, STEPHEN, a merchant in Barbados in 1648. [CLRO.Deposition.3]

NOELL, THOMAS, a merchant in Barbados in 1648. [CLRO.Deposition.3]

NORRIS, JOHN, from Bristol, an indentured servant bound via Bristol for Barbados in December 1658. [BRO]

NORTH, THOMAS, died in Barbados, Admin., 1652, PCC

NOY, HESTER, with two children, in St Michael's, Barbados, in 1680. [HOT.450]

NOY, ISACC, with six children, in St Michael's, Barbados, in 1680. [HOT.450]

NOYES, NICHOLAS, from Hampshire, an indentured servant bound via Bristol for Barbados in December 1658. [BRO]

NUNES, BEATRICE, daughter of Sarah Nunes. [Bridgetown gravestone]

NUNES, BENJAMIN ISRAEL, in Bridgetown, 1772. [BDA.Levy]

NUNES, DAVID P., born 26 April 1790, son of Phineas Nunes, died 23 April 1802. [Bridgetown gravestone]

NUNES, ESTHER, in Bridgetown, 1772. [BDA.Levy]

NUNES, ISAAC ISRAEL, in Bridgetown, 1772. [BDA.Levy]; died 1802. [Bridgetown gravestone];

NUNES, JACOB FRANCE, with four children, in St Michael's, Barbados, in 1680. [HOT.449]; Jacob Franco Nunes, born 1646, a merchant in Barbados, died 22 October 1726. [Bridgetown gravestone]

NUNES, JACOB ISRAEL, born 1731, died 10 January 1797. [Bridgetown gravestone]

NUNES, MOSES, in Bridgetown, 1772. [BDA.Levy]

NUNES, PHINEAS, in Bridgetown, 1772. [BDA.Levy]

NUNES, PHINEAS, born 1771, died 1 February 1825. [Bridgetown gravestone]

NUNES, REBECCA, in Bridgetown, 1772. [BDA.Levy]

NURSE, Mrs, widow of John Nurse, died on Kirton Plantation in March 1824. [The Barbadian.ii]

NUSUM, SAMUEL, died in Bridgetown in April 1824. [The Barbadian.ii]

NUTTALL, THOMAS, from Barbados aboard the Happy Return, master Isaac Rand, bound for London on 14 October 1679. [TNA]

OBEDIENTE, ABRAHAM, with two children, in St Michael's, Barbados, in 1680. [HOT.450]

O'BRYAN, JOHN, born 1759, from Barbados, died in Bristol on 20 September 1813. [GM.83.403]

OGLE, JOHN, from Barbados aboard the ketch Mary and Sarah, master George Conway, bound for Providence on 20 November 1679. [TNA]

OLDRIDGE, ABELL, from Barbados aboard the Hopewell, master William Murphy, bound for Antigua on 10 November 1679. [TNA]

OLTON, DURBAN FREDERICK JENNINGS, born 1839, son of Elizabeth Ann Olton, died 3 July 1861. [St Michael's MI]

OLTON, JOHN ALLEN, died in Barbados on 1 August 1810. [GM.80.387]

OLTON, ORMOND G., born 17 December 1850, died 29 July 1873. [St Andrew's gravestone]

OLTON, O., eldest daughter of John Allen Olton of Harrow Place, Barbados, married Captain William Whitmore, ADC to Major General Munro, in Cabbage Tree Hall, Barbados, on 14 April 1811. [GM.81.589]

OLTON, Mrs, widow of George Olton, died in January 1825. [The Barbadian iii]

O'NEAL, ANN, from Barbados aboard the sloop <u>Rutter,</u> master Edward Duffield, bound for Jamaica on 2 October 1679. [TNA]

O'NEAL, ELIZABETH, infant daughter of T.W.O'Neal, died on Fellowship Estate in July 1825. [The Barbadian iii]

O'NEAL, MARY ANN, second daughter of Thomas Whitfoot O'Neal in Barbados, married Henry Charles Benyon, only son of Robert Cutts Carton a Captain in the Royal Navy, in Devon, in Cheltenham on 1 July 1845. [GM.ns.24.415]

ORDERSON, Dr, minister of St George in 1824. [The Barbadian ii]

ORDERSON, Mrs, born 1779, wife of J W Orderson in Barbados, died on passage to England on 20 July 1810. [GM.80.189][St Michael's MI]

ORGAN, JEREMIAH, of <u>HM Sloop Fowey of Barbados</u> probate, 15 October 1803, PCC. [TNA.Prob.11.1400.112]

OSBORNE, RICHARD, a planter in Barbados, probate, 1653, PCC; also, his wife Mary, probate, 1653, PCC

OSBORNE, ROBERT, a servant of Richard Lilburne, from Barbados aboard the ketch <u>Mary and Sarah,</u> master George Conway, on 24 November 1679. [TNA]

OSBORN, ROBERT, married Sally Hopkins, eldest daughter of John Hopkins of Ingastone Hall, Essex, in Barbados, on 18 September 1741. [GM.11.499]

OSBORNE, SAMUEL, in Barbados, died on 2 August 1767. [GM.37.430]

OSTRAHAN, JOSEPH, born 1759, died 7 August 1809, husband of Elvira, born 61, died 12 January 1848, parents of Reverend Joseph Duncan Ostrehan and Lucretia Gittens. [St Michael's MI]

OUGHTERSON, ARTHUR, from Barbados aboard the <u>Barton</u> bound for England on 6 August 1824. [The Barbadian ii]

OWEN, WILLIAM, born 1612, bound from London aboard the Hopewell to Barbados in February 1635. [TNA.E157.20]

PACHECO, JACOB, with five children, in St Michael's, Barbados, in 1680. [HOT.450]

PACHECO, REBECAH, with two children, in St Michael's, Barbados, in 1680. [HOT.450]

PACKER, JAMES, died in Barbados on 29 January 1859, husband of Ellen Darling, who died in Edinburgh on 15 May 1900. [St Michael's MI]

PACKER, JOHN CUTTING, born 2 May 1777, died 6 December 1856, husband of Martha ...., born 1775, died 18 May 1841. [St Michael's MI]; master of the Central School was appointed supervisor of all schools in town established by the Bishop, in August 1825. [The Barbadian iii]

PAGE, JOHN, a servant of Colonel Christopher Codrington, from Barbados aboard the barque Dove, master Anthony Jenour, bound for Nevis on 29 October 1679. [TNA]

PAIRMAN, JAMES, born 1782, former Postmaster General of Barbados, died there on 6 December 1845. [GM.ns.25.335]

PALACHE, MORDECAI, with one child, in St Michael's, Barbados, in 1680. [HOT.450]

PALLISTER, JAMES, born 1607, bound from London aboard the Hopewell to Barbados in February 1635. [TNA.E157.20]

PALMER, MARY, a spinster, an indentured servant bound via Bristol to Barbados in December 1660. [BRO]

PALMES, BRYAN, born 1811 in Yorkshire, Captain of the 52nd Light Infantry, died in Barbados on 16 December 1839. [St Paul's MI]

PARGITER, THEODORE, died in Mellifont, County Louth, trading with Barbados, probate, 1656, PCC

PARIS, DAVID, born 1725, a merchant in Bristol, aboard the No Account, bound via Bristol, for Barbados in March 1774; also, aboard the Barbados Packet, bound via Bristol for Barbados in November 1775. [TNA.T47.9/11]

PARRIS, OWEN, from Barbados aboard the barque Resolution, master Thomas Gilbert, bound for Antigua on 27 November 1679. [TNA]

PARKER, JOHN, a servant of Colonel Christopher Codrington, from Barbados aboard the barque Dove, master Anthony Jenour, bound for Nevis on 29 October 1679. [TNA]

PARRIS, JAMES WILLIAM, of Ashford, born 1 November 1815, died 20 July 1908, husband of Susanna......, born 7 January 1816, died 20 February 1883. [St Thomas gravestone]

PARRIS, OWEN, from Barbados aboard the barque Joseph, master Stephen Clay, bound for 'Saltertudos' on 21 March 1679. [TNA]

PARRY, CONSTANCE LOUISA, fifth daughter of Thomas Parry the Bishop of Barbados, married John Thomas Dalyell, a Major of the21st North British Fusiliers, son of Lieutenant Colonel Thomas Dalyell of the 42nd Native Infantry, in Barbados on 7 February 1861. [GM.ns.2/10.567]

PARSONS, FRANCIS, from Barbados aboard the Concord, master James Strutt, bound for London on 8 May 1679. [TNA]

PARTRIDGE, ..., son of Samuel T. Partridge MD, was born on Walker's Estate, St George, on 1 January 1824. [The Barbadian.ii]

PARTRIDGE, MARY JULIA, born 1807, wife of S. T. Partridge MD in Barbados, died in Bath in 1830. [GM.100.647]

PASSALAIGNE, PETER, a planter in the parish of St Michael's, Barbados, probate, 26 August 1719, PCC. [TNA.Prob.11.570.73]

PATY, ELIZA, from Barbados aboard the Judith, master Robert Kingsland, bound for London on 13 January 1679. [TNA]

PAYNE, Reverend WILLIAM M., Rector of St Andrew's and Chaplain to the House of Assembly, died in May 1825. [The Barbadian, iii]

PAYNE, Mrs, widow of John Payne of Dodds, Barbados, died in Oldham on 9 April 1810. [GM.80.493]; their daughter died in Oldham on 2 March 1814. [GM.84.812]

PAYNTER, PAUL, a merchant in Aldersgate, London, settled in Barbados by October 1659. [CLRO.Deposition.9]

PEACOCK, BENJAMIN, died 1757 in Barbados. [GM.27.531]

PEAD, THOMAS, from Barbados aboard the ketch Swallow, master Joseph Hardy, bound for Rhode Island on 1 April 1679. [TNA]

PEARSHOUSE, CHESTER, from Barbados aboard the pink Rebecca, master Thomas Williams, bound for Virginia on 22 July 1679. [TNA]

PEARSON, JOHN, from Barbados aboard the Samuel, master John Clarke, bound for London on 28 February 1679. [TNA]

PECHEY, LAMBERT, from Barbados aboard the Ruth, master William Taylor, bound for London on 17 June 1679. [TNA]

PECKETT, JAMES, born 1725, a gentleman from Bath, via Bristol aboard the Eleanor, bound for Barbados in December 1775. [TNA.T47.9/11]

PEERS, RICHARD, in Barbados, probate, 14 April 1662, [TNA.Prob.11.308.173]

PEIXOTTO, ABRAHAM, in Bridgetown, 1772. [BDA.Levy]

PELING, RICHARD, born 1686, son of George Peling a shoemaker in Chester, an indentured servant bound via Liverpool for Barbados in 1702. [LRO]

PEMBERTON, JAMES, a merchant, died 29 June 1736. [St Michael's MI]

PEMMELL, THOMAS, from Barbados aboard the Rose and Crown, master Thomas Crofts, bound for London on 19 May 1679. [TNA]

PENDLETON, MARY, from Barbados aboard the Trent, master George Munjoy, bound for Boston on 8 September 1679. [TNA]

PENNIMAN, ..., from Barbados aboard the Honor, master Thomas Warren, bound for London on 22 April 1679. [TNA]

PERCH, SARAH ELIZABETH, eldest daughter of Thomas Perch in Barbados, married James Bedford of Lougharne, South Wales, son of Colonel Perch of the Bengal Army, in Bath on 3 February 1864. [GM.ns.2/26.380]

PERERA, ISAAC, with two children, in St Michael's, Barbados, in 1680. [HOT.449]

PERERA, ISAAC, with six children, in St Michael's, Barbados, in 1680. [HOT.450]

PERKINN, MARTIN, born 1615, bound from London aboard the Hopewell to Barbados in February 1635. [TNA.E157.20]

PERKINS, CHARLOTTE, second daughter of John Perkins of Blechingly, Surrey, was drowned on passage from Barbados aboard the Atlas on 27 August 1809. [GM.79.1235]

PERKINS, MARIANNE, second daughter of A T Perkins in London, married W J Evans MD, in Barbados on 1 February 1838. [GM.ns.9.539]

PERRIN, MARGARET, from Barbados aboard the Arthur, master Henry Cooker, bound for London on 3 March 1679. [TNA]

PERROT, JAMES LEIGH, from North Leigh, Oxford, married Miss Warkham, in Barbados on 9 October 1764. [GM.34.498]

PERSIVAL, ANDREW, from Barbados aboard the Anne and Jane, master Richard Ratford, bound for London on 23 December 1679. [TNA]

PERWIDGE, JOB, from Barbados aboard the Expedition, master John Harding, bound for Virginia on 5 March 1679. [TNA]; aboard the Endeavour, master James Gilbert, bound for London on 28 March 1679. [TNA]

PHIBBS.ORMSBY, born 1806, Lieutenant Colonel of the 88th Regiment, died in Barbados on 17 January 1848. [St Paul's MI]

PHILLIPS, ABEL, married Miss Evelyn, daughter of Charles Evelyn, in June 1825. [The Barbadian iii]

PHILLIPS, ANN SISUM, daughter of Peter Phillips in Barbados, married George Geoffrey Wyatville, son of Jeffrey Wyatville of Windsor, in London on 17 January 1828. [GM.98.80]

PHILLIPS, ELIAZER, from Barbados aboard the Providence, master Timothy Pront, bound for Boston on 28 June 1679. [TNA]

PHILLIPS, JOANNA OSBORNE, second daughter of Peter Phillips, married W. Gittens Wilson from Bristol, in St Michael's on 14 February 1824. [The Barbadian.ii]

PHILLIPS, JOHN RANDALL, of Lamberts, Barbados, born 1759, died in Torquay, Devon, on 9 September 1845. Elizabeth Went Lovell, his wife, born 1780, daughter of Phillip Lovell, died in Edinburgh on20 July 1831. [St Michael's MI]

PHILLIPS, PHILIP LOVELL, MD, of Lamberts and Durants Estates, born 1806, son of John Randal Phillips, died 2 July 1869. [St Lucy's MI]

PHILLIPS, WILLIAM, died in Barbados, Admin., 1658, PCC

PHILLIPS, WILLIAM, in Barbados, was appointed an attorney in October 1659. [CLRO.Deposition,9]

PHILPOTT, PHILLIP, born 1605, bound from London aboard the Hopewell to Barbados in February 1635. [TNA.E157.20]

PICKERING, Sir HENRY, in Barbados, probate, 27 October 1705. [TNA.Prob.11.484.458]

PICKFORD, ROBERT, from Barbados aboard the ketch Neptune, master Joseph Knott, bound for Virginia on 19 August 1679. [TNA]

PICKFORD, ROBERT, from Barbados aboard the Pearl, master Edward Peirson, bound for the Leeward Islands on 4 September 1679. [TNA]

PICORD, CHARLES, from Barbados aboard the Society, master Edmond Ditty, bound for Bristol on 24 May 1679. [TNA]

PIDDING, PRISCILLA, from Taynton, Gloucestershire, an indentured servant bound via Bristol for Barbados in December 1658. [BRO]

PIDDOCK, WILLIAM, from Barbados aboard the Friends Adventure, master Edward Blades, bound for London on 25 April 1679. [TNA]

PIERCE, ANN, wife of John Bertles, died in Bridgetown on 1 March 1824. [The Barbadian.ii]

PIERCE, Mrs, wife of Thomas E. Pierce the Deputy Purveyor of Hospitals, died in October 1824. [The Barbadian ii]

PIERREPOINT, CHARLOTTE, born 1800, daughter of Thomas Pierrepoint, wife of Henry Crichlow in Barbados, died in England on 10 October 1839. [St Michael's MI]

PIERREPOINT, ..., son of Thomas Pierrepoint, was born in November 1824. [The Barbadian ii]

PIGGOTT, JEAN, born 1688, died 21 April 1733, daughter of Roger and Jean Piggott, and wife of Thomas Wood. [St Thomas MI]

PIGGOTT, Reverend JOSEPH THOMAS, born 1808, died 9 August 1868. [Christ Church MI]

PIGGOTT, Mrs, died in St James in February 1824. [The Barbadian.ii]

PILE, EDWARD, from Barbados aboard the Hope master John Prill, bound for New England on 15 September 1679. [TNA]

PILE, RICHARD PARRIS, born 1776, died in 1824. [The Barbadian ii]

PILE, SARAH BURCHALL, eldest daughter of Conrad Pile, married Robert Cruden Gordon from St Lucia in December 1824. [The Barbadian ii]

PILE, WILLIAM, from Barbados aboard the barque <u>Susanna,</u> master Hugh Babell, bound for Carolina on 13 March 1679. [TNA]

PILE, ..., daughter of Conrade Pile, was born in Brighton, St George, in August 1825. [The Barbadian iii]

PILGRIM, Reverend JOHN F., of St James church in 1824. [The Barbadian ii]

PILGRIM, JOHN, born 1652, a Member of HM Council, died 5 December 1715. [St Michael's MI]

PINDER, ANNE ISABELLA, born 1818, daughter of F. F. Pinder in Barbados, died in Bath on 20 August 1835. [GM.ns.4.444]

PINDER, ELIZABETH, born 1779, daughter of W. Senhouse, the Surveyor General for Customs in the West Indies, and wife of F. F. Pinder in Barbados, died in Bath on 30 December 1836. [GM.ns.7.221]

PINDER, Mrs THOMASINA, widow of J. Pinder, daughter of General Haynes, married Lieutenant C F Lardy of the 4th Regiment, in Barbados on 4 December 1823. [GM.94.456]

PINDER, Reverend WILLIAM LUKE, from Barbados, married Harriet, youngest daughter of Reverend Dr Charles Wilson, Professor of Church History at the University of St Andrews, in Edinburgh, on 8 June 1808. [GM.78.556]

PINDER, WILLIAM M., and family, arrived in Barbados from London aboard the <u>Frances</u> from Liverpool in July 1824. [The Barbadian.ii]

PINDER, ..., son of Reverend John H. Pinder, was born on Hothersal Estate in August 1824. [The Barbadian ii]

PINFOLD, CHARLES, born 1708, former Governor of Barbados, died in London on 24 November 1788. [GM.58.1127]

PINHEIRO, AARON, born 1739, a merchant in Barbados, died 30 January 1795. [Bridgetown gravestone]; in Bridgetown, 1772. [BDA.Levy]

PINHEIRO, Mrs HANNAH, died 1818. [Bridgetown gravestone]

PINHEIRO, ISAAC, born 1722, a merchant in Barbados, died 9 November 1796. [Bridgetown gravestone]; in Bridgetown, 1772. [BDA.Levy]

PINHEIRO, ISAAC, died 1804. [Bridgetown gravestone]

PINHEIRO, JACOB, died 1803. [Bridgetown gravestone]; in Bridgetown, 1772. [BDA.Levy]

PINHEIRO, JAEL, died 1831. [Bridgetown gravestone]

PINHEIRO, LUNAH, died 1821. [Bridgetown gravestone]; in Bridgetown, 1772. [BDA.Levy]

PINHEIRO, RACHEL, in Bridgetown, 1772. [BDA.Levy]

PINKE, JOHN, from Barbados aboard the ketch Prosperous, master David Fogg, bound for Virginia on 2 May 1679. [TNA]

PIPER, WILLIAM, from Barbados aboard the Beginning, master Thomas Blessinger, bound for Virginia on 3 March 1679. [TNA]

PITMAN, EDWARD, born 1795, Assistant Commissary General, died in Barbados on 18 September 1817. [GM.17.561]

PLATT, JOHN, from Barbados aboard the ketch Joseph, master Abraham Knott, bound for New York on 16 June 1679. [TNA]

PLUMER, JOHN, from Barbados aboard the barque Mayflower, master Edward Hubbard, bound for Providence on 5 April 1679. [TNA]

POLEGREEN, JOHN, from Barbados aboard the Honor, master Thomas Warren, bound for London on 16 April 1679. [TNA]

POLLARD, JOSEPH, from Barbados aboard the pink Trent, master George Munjoy, bound for Boston on 1 September 1679. [TNA]

POLLARD, Mrs M., born 1664, died in Barbados in 1779. [GM.49.566]

POLLARD, Mrs, widow of Dr Pollard in Barbados, died in London on 11 November 1808. [GM.78.1128]

PONSFORD, ..., son of Reverend W. Ponsford a military chaplain, was born at Airey Cottage, Barbados, on 6 April 1865. [GM.ns.2/18.775]

POOLE, ANN, born 1684, died in January 1740. [St Andrew's MI]

POOR, MARY, a servant of William Bulkley, from Barbados aboard the ketch Neptune, master Joseph Knott, bound for Virginia on 18 August 1679. [TNA

POOR, MILES, from Barbados aboard the ketch Dove, master John Grafton, bound for Antigua on 29 July 1679. [TNA]

POPE, CHARLES, from Barbados aboard the Honor, master Thomas Warren, bound for London on 22 April 1679. [TNA]

POPHAM, S. T., Colonel and Quartermaster General of Barbados, born 1773, died 25 December 1823, also his daughter Honora Alicia Lambart Popham, born 1803, died at Collymore House, Barbados, on 5 December 1820. [St Michael's MI][GM.91.185]

POPKIN, MICHAEL, an indentured servant, bound via Bristol for Barbados in 1658. [BRO]

POPPLE, MAGNUS, from Barbados aboard the sloop Endeavour, master Thomas Shaw, bound for Carolina on 11 October 1679. [TNA]

PORTMAN, CHRISTOPHER, from Barbados aboard the sloop Endeavour, master Thomas Shaw, bound for Carolina on 11 October 1679. [TNA]

POSLETT, RICHARD, from Barbados aboard the Conclusion, master William Beeding, bound for London on 28 April 1679. [TNA]

POTTLE, CHRISTOPHER, from Barbados aboard the pink Diamond, master Ezekiah Vass, bound for Topsham on 13 May 1679. [TNA]

POVEY, WILLIAM, Provost Marshall of Barbados, in 1658. [CLRO.M8]

POWELL, ARTHUR, from Barbados aboard the Friendsip, master John Williams, bound for London on 8 August 1679. [TNA]

POWELL, DANIEL, of Curmer, bound for Barbados in 1634. [TNA.157.16]

POWELL, MARY, a spinster from Monmouth, an indentured servant bound for Barbados in November 1659. [Gloucestershire Record Office. C.10/2]

POWELL, WILLIAM, a husbandman from Gloucester, an indentured servant bound for Barbados in December 1659. [Gloucestershire Record Office.C10.2]

POWER, CHARLES H., died on 7 November 1825. [The Barbadian iii]

POYER, MARIA JANE, widow of John P. Poyer in Barbados, married Reverend Thomas Griffith Connell from Barbados, in Windsor on 1 September 1853. [GM.ns.40.626]

PREETT, JACOB, with one child, in St Michael's, Barbados, in 1680. [HOT.449]

PRESTON, PLUNKETT STANDISH LYNE, a merchant in Bridgetown, Barbados, married Rachael Susan Grayfoot, daughter of John Grayfoot in Bridgetown, Barbados, on 3 January 1846. [GM.ns.25.421]

PRETTEJOHN, JOHN, of Barbados, married Augusta Buckley on 23 November 1801. [GM.71.1209]

PRETTEJOHN, JOHN, born1730, died in Barbados on 29 June 1803. [GM.73.882]

PRETTEJOHN, JOHN, of Barbados and Harehatch, Berkshire, married Laura Cole, youngest daughter of Charles Cole of Paston Hall, Northamptonshire, on 8 April 1840. [GM.ns.13.536]

PRETTEJOHN, JOHN, a merchant in St Michael's, Barbados, probate, 5 September 1833. [TNA.Prob.11.1821.469]

PRETTEJOHN, Miss, daughter of John Prettejohn jr., in Barbados, was born in Bath on 19 August 1802. [GM.72.778]; and another daughter was born there on 29 July 1803. [GM.73.787]

PRICE, SARAH, in Barbados, probate 25 November 1768, PCC. TNA, [Prob.11.943.347]

PRICHARD, ..., from Beaumaris, an indentured servant, bound via Liverpool to Barbados in May 1698. [LRO]

PRICE, JOHN, from Barbados aboard the Bachelor, master Roger Bagg, bound for Bristol on 14 May 1679. [TNA]

PRICKETT, MARGARET MARY SALTER, in Barbados, probate, 16 May 1799. [TNA.Prob.111.1324.150]

PRIMATT, HUMPHRY, from Barbados aboard the Honor, master Thomas Warren, bound for London on 16 April 1679. [TNA]

PRIOR, PETER, from Denbighshire, an indentured servant, bound via Liverpool for Barbados in July 1698. [LRO]

PRYOR, SAMUEL, a saddler in Barbados, in 1658. [CLRO.Deposition.9]

PROBY, Miss, daughter of the Dean of Lichfield, died aboard the Atlas when on her passage to Bristol from Barbados on 6 August 1804. [GM.74.790]

PROSSER, THOMAS, born 1615, bound from London aboard the Hopewell to Barbados in February 1635. [TNA.E157.20]

PULSOVER, NICHOLAS, a bachelor, died in Barbados, Admin., 1655, PCC

PYNE, SYMON, in Barbados, 1656, [see the will of his brother John Pyne in London], probate, 1656, PCC

PYOTT, ALEXANDER, a gentleman in Barbados, probate, 14 January 1651, PCC. [TNA.Prob.11.215.80]

PYOTT, MARIE, a widow in Barbados, probate, 14 January 1651, [TNA.Prob.11.215.79]

QAY, ABRAHAM, with two children, in St Michael's, Barbados, in 1680. [HOT.449]

QUARK, JOHN, a servant of Thomas Allen, from Barbados aboard the ketch William and Susan, master Ralph Parker, bound for New England on 13 March 1679. [TNA]

QUINTYNE, RICHARD, from Barbados aboard the barque Plantation, master Aser Sharpe, bound for Carolina on 12 August 1679. [TNA]

RADLEY, JAMES, died in Barbados, Admin., 1655, PCC

RAINEY, LUKE, a servant of Henry Applewhite, from Barbados aboard the ketch Prosperous, master David Fogg, bound for Virginia on 6 May 1679. [TNA]

RAINSFORD, EDWARD, from Barbados aboard the William and John, master Samuel Legg, bound for Boston on 28 May 1679. [TNA]

RAMSAY, ANN, second daughter of Nathaniel Thomas Ramsay in Barbados, married Robert Henry, fifth son of Joseph Henry of Dublin, in London on 10 November 1853. [GM.ns.41.185]

RAMSAY, JAMES K., died at Grasett's in November 1825. [The Barbadian iii]

RAMSEY, SAMUEL, sr., born 1754, died 29 July 1813. [St George's MI]

RANKIN, Mr and Miss, arrived in Bridgetown in February 1825 aboard the Concord from Bristol. [The Barbadian iii]

RAVENSCROFT, BENJAMIN, from Barbados aboard the Rose and Crown, master Thomas Crofts, bound for London on 19 May 1679. [TNA]

RAWLINS, STEPHEN, born 1778, son of John Rawlins in Yeovil, Somerset, died in Barbados on 18 August 1803. [GM.73.987]

READ, JAMES, born 1616, bound from London aboard the Hopewell to Barbados in February 1635. [TNA.E157.20]

READ, JOHN, a widower in Barbados, Admin., 1652, PCC

READING, EDWARD, a merchant bound for Barbados in 1648. [CLRO.Deposition.2]

REDDIN, KATHERINE, a servant of Martin Haynes, from Barbados aboard the barque Adventure, master Edward Duffield, bound for Virginia on 3 November 1679. [TNA]

REDMAN, REYNOLD ALLEYNE, born 1819, manager of Hanover Estate, died 24 May 1867. [Christ Church MI]

REECE, BEZSIN KING, born 1765, died 23 September 1838. [St Michael's MI]

REECE, BEZSIN, died at sea aboard the Dee bound from Barbados to England on 22 September 1842. [St Michael's MI]

REECE, SARAH ISABELLA, daughter of R. Reece in Barbados, and wife of Reverend J. C. Corlette, died in Illawarra, New South Wales, Australia, on 28 October 1863. [GM.ns.2/16.262]

REECE, THOMAS, born in 1737, died in St Thomas in August 1825. [The Barbadian iii]

REED, BAYNES, from Barbados, graduated MD at Edinburgh University in 1825. [EMG]

REID, Mrs, died in Bridgetown in July 1824. [The Barbadian.ii]

REMNANT, JAMES, and his wife Joan, from Barbados aboard the Industry, master James Porter, bound for Bristol on 30 April 1679. [TNA]

RENNELL, WILLIAM, infant son of the Bishop of Barbados, and grandson of the Dean of Winchester, died 1827 in Barbados. [GM.97.285]

REYNOLD, HENRY, from St Mellons, Monmouth, an indentured servant bound via Bristol for Barbados in December 1658. [BRO]

RHODES, Mr, of Barbados, died in Bath in October 1761. [GM.21.538]

RICE, JOHN, and JAMES, from Barbados aboard the Young William master Thomas Cornish, bound for Virginia on 3 August 1679. [TNA]

RICH, CHARLES, a merchant in Barbados, probate, 1658, PCC

RICH, ROBERT, sr., from Barbados aboard the Amity, master Benjamin Groves, bound for London on 28 May 1679. [TNA]

RICH, ROBERT, from Barbados aboard the Postilion, master John Praul, bound for New York on 15 August 1679. [TNA]

RICHARD, JAMES, from Barbados aboard the Rebecca, master Thomas Williams, bound for Virginia on 21 July 1679. [TNA]

RICHARDS, THOMAS, born 1616, bound from London aboard the Hopewell to Barbados in February 1635. [TNA.E157.20]

RICHARDSON, JOHN, of Canon Hill, Barbados, Admin., 1649, PCC

RICHARDSON, WILLIAM, born 1754, a gentleman from London aboard the Marshall, bound for Barbados in April 1774. [TNA.T47.9/11]

RICHBELL, RICHARD, from Barbados aboard the sloop Experiment, master Allen Cook, bound for London on 13 May1679. [TNA]

RICHBELL, ROBERT, from Barbados aboard the William and John, master Samuel Legg, bound for Boston on 28 May 1679. [TNA]

RICHBELL, ROBERT, from Barbados aboard the Providence, master Timothy Prout, bound for Boston on 1 July 1679. [TNA]

RICKETTS, ..., Governor of Barbados, letters, 1794-1795.[NRS.GD46.17.13]

RICKETTS, Miss, only daughter of Governor Ricketts of Barbados, married Stanlake Batson in Winfield, Berkshire, on 14 September 1818. [GM.88.274]

RIDLEY, GEORGE, from Barbados aboard the sloop Rutter, master Edward Duffield, bound for Jamaica on 2 April 1679. [TNA]

RIDLEY, THOMAS, a bachelor, who died in Barbados, Admin., 1657, PCC

RISSON, JUDITH, with four children, in St Michael's, Barbados, in 1680. [HOT.449]

ROACH, JOSEPH WATERMAN, born 3 January 1827, died 5 February 1899. [St Michael's MI]

ROACH, WILLIAM, Secretary of the Ancient Samaritan Charitable Society in September 1825. [The Barbadian iii]

ROANE, BANCKS, from Barbados aboard the sloop Hunter, master Walter Assueros, bound for Surinam on 3 March 1679. [TNA]

ROBERTS, HUMPHREY, from Cardiganshire, an indentured servant, bound via Liverpool for Barbados in July 1698. [LRO]

ROBERTS, JOHN, son of Edward Roberts in Queekley, an indentured servant bound via Liverpool for Barbados in 1698. [LRO]

ROBERTS, MAURICE, from Denbighshire, an indentured servant bound via Liverpool for Barbados in 1698. [LRO]

ROBERTS, WILLIAM, from Barbados aboard the pink Endeavour, master James Gilbert, bound for London on 26 March 1679. [TNA]

ROBINSON, ALEXANDER, from Barbados aboard the Mary and Ann, master John Johnson, bound for Antigua on 12 March 1679. [TNA]

ROBINSON, JOSEPH, a merchant in Barbados in 1657, deposition, 1660. [CLRO.Deosition.10]

ROBOTHAM, RICHARD, a bachelor who died in Barbados, Admin., 1650, PCC.

ROBOTHAM, WILLIAM, a servant of Colonel Samuel Newton, from Barbados aboard the Joseph, master Stephen Clay, bound for New York on 4 September 1679. [TNA]

ROBSON, PHENICE, a mariner from Newcastle-on-Tyne, bound for Guinea and Barbados aboard the Civil Society of London, Captain Hewitt, probate 1653, PCC

ROCK, Mrs ANN, born 17 May 1783, died 2 May 1870. [St Lucy's gravestone]

RODRIGUS, ANTHONY, with three children, in St Michael's, Barbados, in 1680. [HOT.449]

ROGERS, WOODS, the Governor of Barbados, died 16 July 1732. [GM.2.979]

ROLLSTONE, Captain SAMUEL, a merchant in Barbados, attorney for Hugh Sowden a merchant in London, 1660. [CLRO.Deposition.10]

ROLLESTON, THOMAS, a merchant from London, bound aboard the Golden Lion of London for Barbados, probate 1654, PCC

ROLLOCK, THOMAS, son of William Rollock of Barbados, died in Jamaica in 1825. [The Barbadian iii]

ROOKESBY, JOHN, a merchant in Barbados, attorney for William Byrd a painter stainer of London in 1660. [CLRO.Deposition.10]

ROOTSEY, THOMAS, of Barbados, a will, 1660. [Essex Record Office, D/DHt.H1]

ROSE, CHRISTOPHER, from Barbados aboard the Patience, master Thomas Hudson, bound for London on 25 February 1679. [TNA]

ROSEMAN, PETER, who died aboard the Sarah in Barbados, Admin., 1657, PCC

ROSS, WILLIAM, from Barbados aboard the ketch William and Susan, master Ralph Parker, bound for New England on 21 March 1679. [TNA]

ROTH, RICHARD, from Barbados aboard the Recovery, master Thomas Chinery, bound for New York on 19 April 1679. [TNA]

ROUS, SAMUEL, was appointed a Councillor of Barbados in 1780. [PC.Col.V.563]; President of Barbados in the 1780s.

ROW, LAWRENCE, from Barbados aboard the Robert, master Nathan Hayman, bound for Boston on 12 April 1679. [TNA]

ROWE, THOMAS, from Wapping, died in Barbados, Admin. 1659, PCC

ROWE, Captain, of the Royal Navy in Barbados, died in Bath in 1819. [GM.88.92]

ROYDEN, WILLIAM, from Barbados aboard the frigate The Constant Warwick, master Ralph Delavall, bound for London on 27 February 1679. [TNA]

RUDGE, THOMAS, from Barbados aboard the briganteen Brothers Adventure, master Robert Darkin, bound for New York on 17 July 1679. [TNA]

RUDLE, ROBERT, from Barbados aboard the John and Henry, master Thomas Cades, bound for Bristol on 15 August 1679. [TNA]

RULE, THOMAS, from Barbados aboard the pink Rebecca, master Thomas Williams, bound for Virginia on 6 May 1679. [TNA]

RUSSELL, FRANCIS, Governor of Barbados, commission, 29 November 1693. [Oxford, Rawl. Ms A449.1b]

RUSSELL, WILLIAM, from Kinsale, an indentured servant, bound via Liverpool to Barbados in June 1698. [LRO]

RUTTER, WILLIAM, from Wellington in Somerset, died in Barbados, Admin. 1660, PCC

RYAN, INGRAM, died on 20 August 1824 [The Barbadian ii]

RYDER, SEYMON, a servant of George Moor, from Barbados aboard the Vineyard, master Henry Perrin, bound for Virginia on 3 March 1679. [TNA]

SACHFIELD, HENRY, a merchant bound for Barbados in 1648. [CLRO.Deposition.2]

SAILES, RICHARD, from Barbados aboard the ketch Swallow, master Joseph Hardy, bound for New England on 29 March 1679. [TNA]

ST CLAIR, WILLIAM, in Barbados, died on 6 June 1757. [GM.27.290]

SALT, SAMUEL, from Barbados aboard the Change, master William King, bound for London on 3 April 1679. [TNA]

SALTER, GEORGE, from Barbados aboard the sloop Hopewell, master William Murphy, bound for Antigua on 7 November 1679. [TNA]

SALTER, RICHARD, from Barbados aboard the ketch William and John, master Samuel Legg, bound for Boston on 29 May 1679. [TNA]

SALTER, RICHARD, born 1710, a Member of HM Council, died 6 August 1776, husband of Margaret Salmon. [St George's MI]

SAMPSON, JOHN, a merchant in Barbados, was appointed an attorney in October 1659. [CLRO.Deposition.9]

SANDERS, BENJAMIN, from Barbados aboard the ketch Beginning, master William Play, bound for New York on 18 March 1679. [TNA]

SANDFORD, JOHN, from Barbados aboard the , Barbados Merchant, master James Cock, bound for Virginia on 1 October 1679. [TNA]

SANDIFORD, HENRY, from Barbados aboard the Robert, master Nathan Hayman, bound for Boston on 12 April 1679. [TNA]

SANDOME, RICHARD, from Barbados aboard the Swallow, master Thomas Withington, bound for Liverpool on 19 May 1679. [TNA]

SARAH, MORDECAH, with four children, in St Michael's, Barbados, in 1680. [HOT.450]

SAUNDERS, Mrs SARAH, died in Bridgetown in March 1825. [The Barbadian iii]

SAVARY, W. T., married Elizabeth Nurse in June 1825. [The Barbadian iii]

SAVARY, Mrs, died in Bridgetown in July 1824. [The Barbadian ii]

SCLATER, WILLIAM SALISBURY, born 1800, from Barbados, died in Greenwich on 12 January 1842. [GM.ns.17.336]

SCOTT, BENJAMIN, from Barbados aboard the Expedition, master John Harding, bound for London on 31 March 1679. [TNA]

SCOTT, SAMUEL, a merchant from London, from Portsmouth aboard the Gibbons, bound for Barbados in January 1776. [TNA.T47.9/11]

SCOTT, THOMAS, from Barbados aboard the pink Rebecca, master Thomas Williams, bound for Virginia on 15 July 1679. [TNA]

SEALY, GEORGE AUGUSTUS, second son of John Sealy the Attorney General of Barbados, married Agnes Senhouse Walker, second daughter of James Walker, in Barbados on 15 November 1866. [GM.ns.3/3.238]

SEALY, HENRY, from Barbados aboard the ketch Neptune, master Joseph Knott, bound for Virginia on 16 August 1679. [TNA]

SEAMAN, THOMAS, from Barbados aboard the Thomas and Sarah, master James Day, bound for London on 22 September 1679. [TNA]

SAER, ELLIOT, born 1690, died 27 March 1756, husband of Jane ....., died 21 April 1761. [St Philip's gravestone]

SEARLE, JOHN, in Barbados, an attorney in October 1659. [CLRO.Depoition.9]

SEARLE, RICHARD, a servant of James Coates, from Barbados aboard the sloop Rutter, master Edward Duffield, bound for Jamaica on 2 October 1679. [TNA]

SEARLE, THOMAS, a merchant from Gloucestershire, late of Barbados, now of London, probate, 1656, PCC

SEAWELL, ELIZABETH, born 1650, wife of Richard Seawell, died 1 September 1728. [Christ Church MI]

SEDGWICK, RALPH, from Barbados aboard the ketch Unity, master James Rainy, bound for Virginia on 3 March 1679. [TNA]

SEGNIOR, JOHN, a bachelor who died in Barbados, Admin., 1658, PCC

SENHOUSE, EDWARD HOOPER, arrived in Barbados from London aboard the Tropic from London in July 1824. [The Barbadian.ii]; born 1788, a Post Captain in the Royal Navy, also Provost Marshal of Barbados, died 22 May 1863. [St Philip's MI]

SENHOUSE, WILLIAM, Surveyor General of Customs of Barbados in 1774, and owner of the Grove Plantation, he died in 1800.

SENIOR, JACOB, from Barbados aboard the barque Dove, master Anthony Jenour, bound for Nevis on 29 October 1679. [TNA]

SENIOR, JOSEPH, with three children, in St Michael's, Barbados, in 1680. [HOT.450]

SERANA, JAELL, with one child, in St Michael's, Barbados, in 1680. [HOT.449]

SERJEANT, RICHARD, from Barbados aboard the <u>Joseph and Ann,</u> master Samuel Evans, bound for Carolina on 14 January 1679. [TNA]

SEWER, JOHN, from Barbados aboard the <u>John and Thomas</u> master Thomas Jenour, bound for Providence on 31 March 1679. [TNA]

SHARPE, MARY, from Barbados aboard the <u>Recovery,</u> master James Browne, bound for Jamaica on 31 December 1679. [TNA]

SHARPE, Colonel WILLIAM, born 1630, died 1683. [St Michael's MI]

SHARP, WILLIAM, in Barbados 1659. [CLRO.Deposition.9]

SHARPLES, ROGER, from Leland, an indentured servant, bound via Liverpool to Barbados in 1698. [LRO]

SHENE, JOSEPH, born 1665, a merchant in Bridgetown, died 20 August 1709. [St Andrew's MI]

SHEPHERD, Mrs ELIZABETH, born 1730, died in October 1825. [The Barbadian iii]

SHEPHERD, Mrs J., in Barbados, died in 1768. [GM.38.143]

SHERLAND, JOHN, from Barbados aboard the <u>Prudence and Mary,</u> master Jacob Green, bound for Boston on 22 May 1679. [TNA]

SHERWIN, JOHN, from Barbados aboard the <u>Ann and Jane,</u> master Richard Ratford, bound for London on 24 December 1679. [TNA]

SHERWOOD, SAMUEL, from Barbados aboard the <u>Two Brothers,</u> master Richard Jeffreys, bound for Jamaica on 13 February 1679. [TNA]

SHERWOOD, ..., son of Lieutenant T. H. Sherwood of the 21st Fusiliers, was born in Barbados on 28 February 1861. [GM.ns.2/10.565]

SHETTERDEN, DRAX, born 1675, died 26 May 1699. [St George's MI]

SHIPTON, HENRY NOBLE, born 1800, son of Reverend John Shipton in Somerset, an Ensign of the King's Own Regiment of Foot, died 5 December 1821. [St Michael's MI]

SHORT, MARTHA, from Barbados aboard the Barbados Merchant, master James Cock, bound for Virginia on 1 October 1679. [TNA]

SHORT, WALTER, from Barbados aboard the Bachelor, master Roger Bagg, bound for Bristol on 12 May 1679. [TNA]

SIBBALD, A., born 1763, from Barbados, died in London on 10 January 1820. [GM. 90.93]

SIDDY, HENRY, from Barbados aboard the barque Adventure, master Edward Duffield, bound for London on 6 November 1679. [TNA]

SIDNEY, JOHN, from Barbados aboard the Laurell, master Robert Oxe, bound for Bristol on 15 December 1679. [TNA]

SILVER, DAVID, in Bridgetown, 1772. [BDA.Levy]

SIMMONS, HENRY PETER, Member of Parliament for St Philip's from 1811 to 1813.

SIMMONS, JOHN ALLEYNE, of Vaucluse, Barbados, married Caroline Gresham, second daughter of Robert Gresham of Bedfordshire, in Campton, Bedfordshire, on 8 February 1855. [GM.ns.43.410]

SIMMONS, PHILIP, Member of Parliament for St Michael's from 1758 until his death in 1774, he was also Treasurer of Barbados and Speaker of the House of Assembly, husband of [1] Rebecca King, and [2] Mary Kirton.

SIMON, HESTER BAR, with five children, in St Michael's, Barbados, in 1680. [HOT.449]

SIMPSON, DONALD, a civil engineer and owner of The Crane Hotel in St Philip in 1886.

SINCKLER, Reverend E. G., incumbent of St Leonard's, Barbados, from 1855 to 1881. [St Leonard's MI]

SINCKLER, JAMES, MD in Barbados, married Maria Jane Patterson, daughter of Captain Theopolius Patterson of the Royal Marines, in London on 5 September 1854. [GM.ns.42.618]; she died in Barbados on 25 October 1855. [GM.ns.456]

SINDRY, JOHN, from Barbados aboard the Recovery, master Samuel Evans, bound for Jamaica on 24 December 1679. [TNA]

SIVEE, JOHN, from St Malo in France, bound aboard the William of London, master John Williams, for Barbados, probate, 1656, PCC

SKAHANE, TEIGE, from Barbados aboard the Industry, master James Porter, bound for Bristol on 14 May 1679. [TNA]

SKEETE, AGNES, niece of William Bishop the Governor of Barbados, married Lieutenant Colonel Bonham of the 69th Regiment, in Bridgetown, Barbados, on 26 February 1800. [GM.70.588]

SKEETE, AGNES BONHAM, third daughter of E. Skeete in Barbados, married S. L. Gower of Little Hempston, Devon, in Wells on 1 September 1840. [GM.ns.14.424]

SKEETE, MARGARET, daughter of J. B. Skeete the President of Brasil, married John C. Russell of Warminster, Wiltshire, in Brighton on 15 December 1864. [GM.ns.2/18.98]

SKEETE, THOMAS, MD, born 1757 in Barbados, died in London in 1789. [GM.59.575]

SKEETE, Mrs, widow of John Braithwaite Skeete in Barbados, died on Mangrove Estate, Barbados, on 26 September 1816. [GM.86.566]

SKINNER, DOROTHY GRIFFITH, born 28 February 1765, daughter of William Rollock, and wife of Isaac Skinner in Barbados, died there on 16 July 1852. [GM.ns.38.655]

SKIRING, RICHARD, a grocer from Southwark, Surrey, bound for Barbados, probate, 1654, PCC

SLAUGHTER, WILLIAM, a servant of John Jennings, from Barbados aboard the Joseph and Ann, master Samuel Evans, bound for Carolina on 14 January 1679. [TNA]

SLINGSBY, HARRY, in Barbados, probate, 6 November 1747. [TNA.Prob.11.758.47]

SLOCOMBE, RUPERT, fourth son of Joseph Slocombe in Stockwell, died in Barbados on 30 June 1852. [GM.ns.38.433]

SLOUGHTER, WILLIAM, a merchant in Barbados, probate, 1649. [PCC]

SMART, JOHN, from Barbados aboard the Ann and Jane, master Richard Ratford, bound for London on 24 December 1679. [TNA]

SMITH, ALICIA, from Barbados, married Thomas Tindall, in Bristol in August 1756. [GM.26.450]

SMITH, EDWARD, from Barbados aboard the barque Susannah, master Hugh Baskell, bound for Carolina on 12 March 1679. [TNA]

SMITH, HESTER, a spinster from Over, Gloucestershire, an indentured servant bound for Barbados in November 1659. [Gloucestershire Record Office. C.10/2]

SMITH, HESTER, from Barbados aboard the Plantation, master Aser Sharpe bound for Carolina on 25 February 1679. [TNA]

SMITH, ISAAC, from Barbados aboard the Supply, master John Meadows, bound for Boston on 14 May 1679. [TNA]

SMITH, JOHN, a servant of Colonel Christopher Codrington, from Barbados aboard the barque Dove, master Anthony Jenour, bound for London on 29 October 1679. [TNA]

SMITH, JOHN, from Barbados aboard the Ann and Jane, master Richard Ratford, bound for London on 22 December 1679. [TNA]

SMITH, JOHN, a mariner in Barbados, probate 12 October 1774, PCC. [TNA.Prob.11.735.400]

120

SMITH, JOHN LUCIE, born 1795, from Demerara, died in Barbados on 10 April 1844. [GM.ns.22.110]

SMITH, MARGARET, a servant of Thomas Doxey, from Barbados aboard the Brothers Adventure, master John Selleck, bound for New York on 26 April 1679. [TNA]

SMITH, PHILIP, from Barbados aboard the Joseph and Ann, master Samuel Evans, bound for Carolina on 14 January 1679. [TNA]

SMITH, RICHARD, from Barbados aboard the ketch Unity, master James Rainy, bound for Virginia on 1 April 1679. [TNA]

SMITH, THOMAS, born 1614, bound from London aboard the Hopewell to Barbados in February 1635. [TNA.E157.20]

SMITH, THOMAS, from Barbados aboard the Bachelor, master William Knott, bound for London on 9 July 1679. [TNA]

SMITH, THURLO, a servant of Henry Sealy, from Barbados aboard the ketch Neptune, master Joseph Knott, bound for Virginia on 16 August 1679. [TNA]

SMITH, WILLIAM, from Barbados aboard the James, master William Sweetland, bound for New York on 28 January 1679. [TNA]

SMITH, WILLIAM, from Barbados aboard the New Concord, master James Strutt, bound for London on 20 May 1679. [TNA]

SMITH, WILLIAM, born 1773, died 27 August 1801, husband of Catherine Sims, born 1773, died 23 April 1800. [St Michael's MI]

SMITTEN, ELIZABETH MARTHA, daughter of Richard and Katherine Smitten, died 31 August 1808, aged 20 months. [St Thomas MI]

SNACKNELL, RICHARD, from Barbados aboard the Nathaniel, master William Clarke, bound for Boston on 28 April 1679. [TNA]

SNELLING, WILLIAM, a merchant in Barbados, an attorney in November 1659. [CLRO.Deposition.9]

SOBER, JOHN, from Barbados, married Penelope Blake, in Sevenoaks, Kent, on 6 November 1760. [GM.30.542]

SOMERFIELD, CHARLES, in Barbados, died on 10 May 1758. [GM.28.244]

SONE, GEORGE, from Barbados aboard the barque Blessing, master Francis Watlington, bound for Bermuda on 16 August 1679. [TNA]

SOUSA, ABRAHAM, with two children, in St Michael's, Barbados, in 1680. [HOT.449]

SOUTHWELL, Reverend HENRY GEORGE, late of Trinity College, Dublin, died in Barbados on 25 February 1854. [GM.ns.41.552]

SOUTHWELL, WILLIAM, Captain of the 31st Regiment of St Michael's, Barbados, probate, 22 April 1807, PCC. [TNA.Prob.11.1460.134]

SOUTHWORTH, FRANCIS, from Barbados aboard the ketch Prosperous, master David Fogg, bound for Virginia on 2 May 1679. [TNA]

SPARKE, JOHN, in Barbados, probate, 6 December 1679, PCC. [TNA.Prob.11.361.411]

SPARKES, SAMUEL, from Barbados aboard the William and John, master Samuel Legg, bound for Boston on 29 May 1679. [TNA]

SPENCER, Mrs ELIZABETH, born 1741, died in August 1825. [The Barbadian iii]

SPENCER, PETER, married Elizabeth Thornhill, daughter of Dowding Thornhill, on 25 November 1824. [The Barbadian ii]; their daughter was born in November 1825. [The Barbadian iii]

SPENCER, JOHN WILLIAM, married Jane, daughter of Dowding Thornhill, on 14 April 1825. [The Barbadian iii]

SPICER, SAMUEL, from Barbados aboard the Hope, master Joseph Ball, bound for London on 22 April 1679. [TNA]

SPITTLE, ROBERT, an indentured servant, bound via Bristol for Barbados in 1658. [BRO]

SPITTLE, ROBERT, from Barbados aboard the sloop Katherine, master Andrew Gall, bound for Antigua on 29 November 1679. [TNA]

SPITTLE, ROGER, an indentured servant, bound via Bristol for Barbados in 1658. [BRO]

SPOONER, JOHN, jr., from Barbados, died in London on 6 April 1819. [GM.88.381]; probate, 18 May 1819, PCC. [TNA. Prob.11.1616.293],

SPRY, WILLIAM, the Governor of Barbados, died in 1772. [GM.42.495]

SRANE, ALMONS, from Barbados aboard the Eliza, master Peter Major, bound for Nevis on 19 April 1679. [TNA]

STACY, WILLIAM, from Barbados aboard the Society master William Gerard, bound for Boston on 11 March 1679. [TNA]

STANLEY, JOHN, a glover, an indentured servant bound via Bristol to Barbados in December 1660. [BRO]

STANFAST, GEORGE, in Bristol and Barbados, will, 1658. [Inst. Latin American Studies, London, C105/27]

STANLEY, ROBERT, from Barbados aboard the Malaga Merchant, master Roger Horner, bound for London on 20 September 1679. [TNA]

STANNAGE, THOMAS, from Barbados aboard the pink Rebecca, master Thomas Williams, bound for Virginia on 15 July 1679. [TNA]

STANTON, PEARCE, from Barbados aboard the barque Resolution, master John Inglebee, bound for Antigua on 10 May 1679. [TNA]

STAPLETON, WALTER, from Barbados aboard the Society, master Edmond Ditty, bound for Bristol on 5 May 1679. [TNA]

STEELE, JOSHUA, a Councillor of Barbados, died there in October 1796. [GM.67.80]; a planter in Barbados, 1798-1799. [NRS.GD46.17.15/18]

STEEL, MARY, from Barbados aboard the <u>Merchant Bonadventure,</u> master William Buckley, bound for New York on 17 February 1679. [TNA]

STEEL, MARY, from Barbados aboard the <u>Supply,</u> master Joseph Freeman, bound for London on 26 March 1679. [TNA]

STEPHEN, NATHANIEL, from Barbados aboard the <u>Recovery,</u> master Thomas Chinnery, bound for New York on 19 April 1679. [TNA]

STEPHENS, SYLVESTER, from Barbados aboard the ketch <u>Nicholas and Rebecca,</u> master Nicholas Blake, bound for New York on 20 May 1679. [TNA]

STEPHENS, ZACHARIAH, born 1718, the Customs Controller in Bridgetown, Barbados, died there on 16 June 1793. [GM.63.768]; probate, 1 April 1794, PCC. [TNA.Prob.11.1244.15]

STEVENS, THEODORE, in Barbados, dead by October 1659. [CLRO.Deposition.9]

STEWART, Colonel, of the 1st West Indian Regiment, died in Barbados on 21 October 1799. [GM.70.283]

STILE, JOSEPH, from Talkell Hill, Staffordshire, an indentured servant, bound via Liverpool to Barbados in 1698. [LRO]

STOAKES, MICHAEL, from Barbados aboard the <u>Society,</u> master William Gerard, bound for Boston on 8 March 1679. [TNA]

STOCKLEY, JOHN, and MARY, from Barbados aboard the <u>Two Brothers,</u> master Richard Jeffrey, bound for Jamaica on 13 February 1679. [TNA]

STONE, JOHN, from Barbados aboard the Bachelor's Delight, master Robert Greenaway, bound for London on 2 August 1679. [TNA]

STRAKER, THOMAS JAMES, born 1782 in Barbados, the Customs Controller of Barbados and St Lucia, died on passage to Lisbon aboard the Duke of Kent on 6 March 1814. [GM.84.412]

STRANGEWAY, PHILLIP, who died in Barbados, Admin., 1651, PCC

STRAUSE, ELIAS, from Barbados aboard the Experiment, master Thomas Airbony, bound for London on 22 July 1679. [TNA]

STRODE, EDWYN, in Barbados, a letter, 30 March 1688. [HMC.53]

SULAVANT, MARTIN, of St Katherine's in Dublin, a mariner aboard HMS Melford in Barbados, probate, 13 April 1705, PCC. [TNA.Prob.11.481.273]

SUTTON, JOHN, from Barbados aboard the Prosperous, master Thomas Woodcock, bound for London on 25 June 1679. [TNA]

SWAIN, CHARLES OLTON, son of Charles Swain, was born on 14 October 1825. [The Barbadian iii]

SWAIN, Reverend, arrived in Bridgetown aboard the Concord from Bristol in February 1825. [The Barbadian iii]

SWAIN, Mr W., arrived in Bridgetown aboard the Concord from Bristol in February 1825. [The Barbadian iii]

SWANLEY, ROBERT, from Barbados aboard the Ann and James, master Richard Ratford, bound for London on 30 December 1679. [TNA]

SWARIS, DAVID, with five children in St Michael's, Barbados, in 1680. [HOT.450]

SWEETING, RICHARD, from Barbados aboard the barque Adventure, master Edward Duffield, bound for London on 3 November 1679. [TNA]

SWIFT, JOHN, a bachelor who died in Barbados, Admin., 1658, PCC

SWINNEY, THOMAS, from Barbados aboard the sloop <u>True Friendship,</u> master Charles Callahan, bound for Antigua on 7 October 1679. [TNA]

SYMONDS, JOHN, of Barbados, probate, 1647, PCC

SYMONS, JOHN, a labourer in Barbados, probate, 1628, PCC. [TNA.Prob.11.154.556]

SYMONS, SAMUEL, from Barbados aboard the <u>James,</u> master William Sweetland, bound for New York on 11 February 1679. [TNA]

TALBOT, HENRY, from Barbados, married Miss Craddock from Bridgenorth, on 3 December 1758. [GM.28.611]

TALERSON, Miss, arrived in Bridgetown aboard the <u>Mercy</u> in February 1825. [The Barbadian iii]

TAPPER, THOMAS, from Barbados aboard the ketch <u>Malaga Merchant</u> master Roger Homer, bound for London on 18 September 1679. [TNA]

TAWYER, ELIZABETH, a widow from Barbados, died in London, probate 1650, PCC

TAYLOR, JOHN, born 1612, bound from London aboard the <u>Hopewell</u> to Barbados in February 1635. [TNA.E157.20]

TAYLER, JOHN, with his wife Joanne, indentured servants bound via Bristol to Barbados in December 1660. [BRO]

TAYLOR, JOHN, jr., born 1800, died on 10 April 1825. [The Barbadian iii]

TAYLOR, MARY, born 1781, wife of Dr Sutton Taylor, died near St Ann's in September 1825. [The Barbadian iii]

TAYLOR, MARY, third daughter of George N Taylor in Barbados, married James R Holligan a barrister, in West Teignmouth on 3 December 1853. [GM.ns.41.308]

TAYLOR, SUTTON, in Bridgetown, Barbados, probate, 28 March 1832. [TNA.Prob.11.1797.433]

TAYLOR, Mrs, wife of John Taylor, died in December 1824. [The Barbadian ii]

TEAGUE, JAMES, of Barbados, died in Ilminster, Somerset, Admin., 1652, PCC

TEAGE, JOHN, from Barbados aboard the Friendship, master John Williams, bound for London on 26 June 1679. [TNA]

TEMPUS, WILLIAM, an indentured servant, bound via Bristol aboard The Dolphin for Barbados in March 1660. [BRO]

TERRY, CHRISTOPHER, jr., from Barbados aboard the Experiment, master Allan Cock, bound for London on 10 May 1679. [TNA]

THAYER, NATHANIEL, from Barbados aboard the Society, master William Guard, bound for Boston on 17 July 1679. [TNA]

THODIE, STEPHEN, died in Barbados, probate, 1658, PCC

THOMAS, ABIGAIL JANE, widow of William Carter Thomas in Barbados, died in Clifton on 7 July 1846. [GM.ns.26.331]

THOMAS, CHARLES, from Usk, Monmouthshire, an indentured servant, bound via Bristol for Barbados in 1658. [BRO]

THOMAS, GEORGE, from Barbados aboard the Prudence and Mary, master Jacob Green, bound for Boston on 24 May 1679. [TNA]

THOMAS, JOHN HENRY, eldest son of Grant E Thomas the President of Barbados, married Elizabeth Williams Murray, youngest daughter of William Murray of the Colonial Bank, in Barbados on 4 July 1865. [GM.ns.2/19.373]

THOMAS, PHILLIP, an indentured servant, bound via Bristol for Barbados in 1658. [BRO]

THOMAS, WILLIAM CARTER, died in Bridgetown in May 1824. [The Barbadian. ii]

THOMAS, Mrs, aged 78, died at the residence of Mrs Morris in Floric on 12 August 1824. [The Barbadian ii]

THOMPSON, CHRISTOPHER, a planter in Barbados, deceased by 1649. [CLRO.Deposition.3]

THOMPSON, Captain EDWARD, died 6 April 1669, and his brother Captain Samuel Thompson, died 18 March 1655. [St Thomas gravestone]

THOMPSON, JAMES, a former planter in Barbados, married L. Watson in London on 13 November 1781. [GM.53.541]

THOMPSON, JANE ANN, born 1781, a 'free coloured woman' died 27 January 1816. [St Andrew's gravestone]

THORNHILL, HENRY, a Councillor of Barbados before 1770. [PC.Col.V.562]

THORNHILL, TIM, born 26 June 1747, died in Barbados on 21 April 1813. [GM.83.660][St George's MI]

THORNHILL, Mrs, died in St James in February 1824. [The Barbadian.ii]

THORNTON, WILLIAM, from Barbados aboard the Friends Adventure, master Edward Blades, bound for London on 25 April 1679. [TNA]

THORPE, GEORGE, in St George, Barbados, died on 8 August 1825, probate, 2 November 1827, PCC. [TNA.Prob;.11.1733.17] [The Barbadian iii]

THORPE, JOHN, from Barbados aboard the sloop Ann and Jane, master Richard Rattford, bound for London on 11 December 1679. [TNA]

TICKELL, WILLIAM, a merchant in Barbados, an attorney in 1658. [CLRO.Dep.10]

TIDY, Mrs, daughter of the late Chief Justice Pinder of Barbados, widow of Colonel Francis Skelly Tidy of the 24th Regiment, died in Portsmouth, Hampshire, on 12 March 1849. [GM.ns.31.666]

TINICO, JACOB, from Barbados aboard the ketch William and John, master Ralph John Sanders, bound for New England on 11 April 1679. [TNA]

TIPPIN, JOHN, from Barbados aboard the frigate Constant Warwick, master Ralph Delavall, bound for London on 1 March 1679. [TNA]

TITE, JAMES, born 1758, a gentleman from Bath, via Bristol aboard the Eleanor, bound for Barbados in December 1775. [TNA.T47.9/11]

TOLLO, DEMENEREZ LEWIS, from Barbados aboard the Bachelor, master William Knott, bound for London on 12 July 1679. [TNA]

TOMLINSON, JOHN, born 1758, from London aboard the Gibbons, bound for Barbados in December 1774, 'to see his father'. [TNA.T47.9/11]

TOOLES, MORGAN, from Barbados aboard the Friends Adventure, master Edward Blades, bound for London on 19 April 1679. [TNA]

TOOLEY, Miss, from London, died in Barbados on 23 May 1799. [GM.69.621]

TOOSEY, MARY, born 1775, died 23 May 1799. [St Michael's MI]

TOPPIN, ROBERT PILGRIM, born 1803, died 15 January 1839, son of Mehetable Morris Toppin, born 1779, died at Clifden near Bristol on 18 December 1840. [St Philip's MI]

TOREZ, JUDIEAH, with two children, in St Michael's, Barbados, in 1680. [HOT.449]

TOWNSEND, RICHARD, from Barbados aboard the Nathaniel, master William Clarke, bound for Boston on 28 April 1679. [TNA]

TRANT, RICHARD, in Barbados, probate, 8 August 1684, PCC. [TNA.Prob.11.377.67]

TRATTLE, WILLIAM, a widower in Barbados, Admin., 1658, PCC

TRAVIS, RICHARD, from Barbados aboard the Fellowship, master Thomas Pim, bound for Antigua on 21 February 1679. [TNA]

TREBLE, PETER, a yeoman, an indentured servant bound via Bristol to Barbados in December 1660. [BRO]

TREMILLS, WILLIAM, from Barbados aboard the sloop Hopewell, master William Murphy, bound for Antigua on 17 November 1679. [TNA]

TREVIS, WILLIAM, in Barbados, Admin. 1652, PCC

TROTMAN, Mrs, wife of Thomas Trotman, from Barbados, died in London in 1793. [GM.63.867]

TULL, WILLIAM M., married Sarah Taitt in St Michael's church in July 1824. [The Barbadian ii]

TURDALL, JOHN, a servant of Henry Sealy, from Barbados aboard the Neptune, master Joseph Knott, bound for Virginia on 16 August 1679. [TNA]

TURNER, ARTHUR, a thief in Bridewell, London bound for Barbados in 1632.

TURNER, JOHN from Barbados aboard the Nathaniel, master William Clarke, bound for Boston on 29 April 1679. [TNA]

TURNER, WILLIAM, a yeoman from Wedmore, Somerset, an indentured servant, bound via Bristol for Barbados in 1658. [BRO]

TURPIN, Mrs MARY JANE, died in July 1824. [The Barbadian ii]

TURPIN, SARAH, born 1790, died 7 October 1863. [Christ Church MI]

USHER, WILLIAM, born 1613, bound from London aboard the Hopewell to Barbados in February 1635. [TNA.E157.20]

VALE, JACOB FONCEDO, with five children, in St Michael's, Barbados, in 1680. [HOT.450]

VALUARDE, ABRAHAM, with two children, in St Michael's, Barbados, in 1680. [HOT.449]

VALVERDE, DAVID, in Bridgetown, 1772. [BDA.Levy]

VALVERDE, JACOB, in Bridgetown, 1772. [BDA.Levy]

VASSALL, WILLIAM, in Barbados, probate, 20 June 1657. [TNA.Prob.11.265.507]

VAUGHTON, JOHN, an estate owner in Barbados, died on 8 November 1754. [GM.24.530]

VAUX, JOHN, from Barbados aboard the Roebuck, master William Shafto, bound for London on 2 May 1679. [TNA]

VEISH, Mr, nephew of John Moore, died in February 1825. [The Barbadian iii]

VERIN, NATHANIEL, from Barbados aboard the pink Rebecca, master Thomas Williams, bound for Virginia on 16 July 1679. [TNA]

VERNON, PETER, from Barbados aboard the Ann and Jane, master Richard Rattford, bound for London on 24 December 1679. [TNA]

VINCENT, MARK, from London, died in Barbados, Admin., 1655, PCC

VINER, ANTHONY, from Barbados aboard the James, master Paul Green, bound for Antigua on 10 March 1679. [TNA]

WADE, ANDREW, of Barbados, died in Demerara on 4 June 1798. [GM.8.811]

WAINWRIGHT, JAMES, from Barbados aboard the Happy Return, master Isaac Rand, bound for London on 17 October 1679. [TNA]

WALCOTT, ROBERT BOWIE, MD, born 1821, died 6 April 1894, husband of Rachel Frances Walcott, born 1823, died 24 February 1894. [St Andrew's MI]

WALFORD, JOHN, a gentleman from London, bound for Barbados, probate, 1647, [PCC]

WALKER, WILLIAM, born 1614, bound from London aboard the Hopewell to Barbados in February 1635. [TNA.E157.20]

WALL, SAMUEL, from Barbados aboard the sloop True Friendship, master Charles Callahan, bound for Antigua on 7 October 1679. [TNA]

WALLINGTON, SAMUEL, from Westbury, an indentured servant, bound via Liverpool to Barbados in 1698. [LRO]

WALROND, BENJAMIN, born 1787, Provost Marshal of Barbados, died there on 16 July 1844. [GM.ns.22.334]; his daughter was born on 29 November 1824. [The Barbadian ii]

WALROND, BENJAMIN, son of the late George Walrond, died in Barbados on 28 September 1851. [GM.ns.37.105]

WALROND, GEORGE, father of a daughter born at Fauxbourg in April 1825. [The Barbadian.iii]

WALROND, NICHOLAS HUMPHREY, from Barbados, died in London on 27 October 1846. [GM.ns.26.664]

WALTHON, JOHN, a cordwainer, an indentured servant bound via Bristol to Barbados in December 1660. [BRO]

WARD, AGNES, wife of Joseph Ward a merchant, died 12 January 1713. [St Michael's MI]

WARD, MARIA, born 1801, wife of William Ward, died 1 November 1829, parents of Maria, born December 1828, died 6 September 1829. [St Michael's MI]

WARD, RICHARD, a surgeon in Barbados, probate, 1660. [PCC]

WARKHAM, Miss, from Barbados, married James Leigh Perrot of North Leigh, in Oxford on 9 October 1764. [GM.34.498]

PEOPLE OF BARBADOS, 1625-1875

WARMINGTON family in Barbados, correspondence from 1863.
[Colonial Records Project, Oxford]

WARNER, NATHANIEL, from Barbados aboard the sloop Unity, master
Lawrence Sluice, bound for Antigua on 6 December 1679. [TNA]

WARREN, ROBERT, in Barbados, a letter, 1721. [Leeds Archives,
TN/C.12/159]

WATERS, WILLIAM O., of the Commissary Department in Barbados,
died there on 15 October 1805. [GM.75.1171]

WATKINS, PHILLIP, from Barbados aboard the Prudence and Mary,
master Jacob Green, bound for Boston on 26 May 1679. [TNA]

WATSON, ADELE, widow of N. J. Watson in Burnopfield, died in
Barbados on 22 April 1854. [GM.ns.42.200]

WATSON, EDWARD SYDNEY, married Sarah Hamden, daughter of
Jarratt Hamden, on 30 December 1824. [The Barbadian ii]

WATSON, ELEANOR, born 1803, died in December 1805. [The
Barbadian iii]

WATSON, MARY, born 1813, wife of William Watson, died 17 May
1841, mother of Sarah Christian Watson, an infant, died 26 October
1834. [St Michael's MI]

WATTS, SAMUEL, from Ramelton, County Donegal, merchant in
Barbados, letters, 1800-1840. [PRONI]

WEBB, JAMES, a yeoman and an indentured servant, bound via
Bristol aboard The Dolphin for Barbados in March 1660. [BRO]

WEBSTER, EDWARD, from Barbados aboard the Nathaniel, master
William Clarke, bound for Boston on 26 April 1679. [TNA]

WEBSTER, HENRY, from Barbados aboard the Robert, master Robert
Hayman, bound for Boston on 15 April 1679. [TNA]

WEEKES, JOHN, died in Barbados, probate, 1654, PCC

WEEKES, NATHANIEL SIMS, born in Barbados in 1740, died at the Cove of Cork on 12 December 1800. [St Philip's MI]

WEEKES, THOMAS, from Totnes, Devon, a planter in Barbados, probate, 23 October 1654, PCC [TNA.Prob.11.241.219]

WELCH, EDMOND, a servant of John Hopcroft, from Barbados aboard the Rebecca, master Thomas Williams, bound for Virginia on 18 July 1679. [TNA]

WELLS, Mrs, wife of Henry B. Wells, died in August 1824. [The Barbadian ii]

WELSH, THOMAS, from Pembroke, an indentured servant bound via Bristol for Barbados in 1660. [BRO]

WELTDEN, ANTHONY, from Barbados aboard the Society, master William Guard, bound for Boston on 10 March 1679. [TNA]

WENT, MARY ELVIRA, eldest daughter of Thomas Went in St Lucy's, Barbados, married William Leacock Jordan, eldest son of William Leacock Jordan, on 16 October 1860. [GM.ns.2/9.661]

WEST, THOMAS, Chief Judge of Barbados, witness to a deed, dated 1 September 1764. [NRS.RD3224/1.9]

WESTBURY, THOMAS, from Barbados aboard the Barbados, master Edward Griffith, bound for the Leeward Islands on 1 September 1679. [TNA]

WESTON, WILLIAM, died in Barbados, Admin., 1655, PCC

WEVILL, ANTHONY, bound for Barbados, probate, 1656, PCC

WHEELER, CHRISTOPHER, from Barbados aboard the Robert, master Richard Cock, bound for London on 28 August 1679. [TNA]

WHEELER, JOHN, jr., from Barbados aboard the Return, master Thomas Harvey, bound for New England on 1 August 1679. [TNA]

WHEELER, WILLIAM, from Barbados aboard the sloop <u>Bachelor,</u> master Peter Swaine, bound for the Leeward Islands on 5 May 1679. [TNA]

WHITAKER, REBECCA, born 1739, a musical instrument maker in London, from London aboard the <u>America,</u> bound for Barbados in July 1774. [TNA.T47.9/11]

WHITAKER, WILLIAM, a gentleman in Barbados, probate, 1656, PCC

WHITAKER, ..., a planter in Barbados, returned aboard the <u>Three Brothers,</u> from Portsmouth to Barbados in March 1776. [TNA.T47.9/11]

WHITE, JAMES, a merchant in Barbados, probate, 11 February 1668, PCC. [TNA.Prob.11.326.211]

WHITE, PAUL, a mariner of Bermondsey, master of the <u>Jacob</u> bound for Barbados in 1625. [CLRO.Deposition.3]

WHITE, WILLIAM, born 1754, a gentleman from London aboard the <u>Marshall,</u> bound for Barbados in April 1774. [TNA.T47.9/11]

WHITEBEAR, JOSEPH, from Barbados aboard the <u>Three Brothers,</u> master Peter Boss, bound for New York on 1 November 1679. [TNA]

WHITECLIFFE, GEORGE, from Barbados aboard the <u>Samaritan,</u> master Valentine Trim, bound for Liverpool on 12 March 1679. [TNA]

WHITFIELD, MATHEW, from Barbados aboard the ketch <u>Prosperous,</u> master David Fogg, bound for Virginia on 2 May 1679. [TNA]

WHITEFOOT, AMOS, from Barbados aboard the <u>Robert,</u> master Nathan Hayman,, bound for Boston on 27 March 1679. [TNA]

WHITLEE, MARY, from Barbados aboard the ketch <u>Beginning,</u> master William Play, bound for New York on19 March 1679. [TNA]

WHITELING, WILLIAM, from Barbados aboard the <u>Francis and Susan,</u> master Philip Knell, bound for Boston on 26 May 1679. [TNA]

WHITEN, ROBERT, an organist in Barbados, probate, 1 July 1748, PCC. [TNA.Prob.11.763.120]

WHITLOCK, JAMES, married Miss Hughes from London in Barbados on 1 July 1773. [GM.43.359]

WICKHAM, BENJAMIN, from Barbados aboard the barque Resolution, master John Inglebe, bound for Antigua on 20 May 1679. [TNA]

WICKHAM, ELIZA, from Barbados aboard the sloop John and Francis, master John Howard, bound for Antigua on 1 September 1679. [TNA]

WICKLOW, PHILIP, from Barbados, died in London on 8 January 1783. [GM.53.94]

WIGNALL, JAMES, a merchant in Barbados, 1660. [CLRO.Deposition.10]

WILDE, WILLIAM, from Barbados aboard the Happy Return, master Isaac Rand, bound for London on 17 October 1679. [TNA]

WILDIE, REBECCA, born 1752, a spinster from London, via London aboard the Britannia, bound for Barbados in October 1774. [TNA.T47.9/11]

WILKINSON, DANIEL, a servant of Robert Hall, from Barbados aboard the barque Resolution, master Daniel Acklin, bound for Providence on 10 April 1679. [TNA]

WILKINSON, GEORGINA, daughter of James Wilkinson in Barbados, married Lieutenant G. G. Phillips of the Royal Navy, in London on 3 August 1852. [GM.ns.38.411]

WILKINSON, Mr, Eversley' arrived in Barbados from London aboard the Tropic from London in July 1824. [The Barbadian.ii]

WILKINS, JOHN, from Barbados aboard the Nathaniel, master William Clarke, bound for Boston on 26 April 1679. [TNA]

WILKS, NATHANIEL, from Barbados aboard the Merchant Adventure, master William Buckley, bound for London on 25 March 1679. [TNA]

WILLIAMS, ARTHUR, from Barbados aboard the sloop Hopewell, master William Murphy, bound for Antigua on 7 November 1679. [TNA]

WILLIAMS, EDWARD THOMAS, married Mary Armstrong Boyce, on 23 August 1825. [The Barbadian iii]

WILLIAMS, MARY ELIZABETH, wife of Edward T. Williams in Bridgetown, died on 6 February 1824. [The Barbadian ii]

WILLIAMS, MATTHEW, from Barbados aboard the Old Head of Kingsale, master Robert Barker, bound for the Leeward Islands on 4 January 1679. [TNA]

WILLIAMS, Mrs PHILLIPA, from Barbados, died in Kingsdown, Somerset, in 1813. [GM.83.668]

WILLIAMS, SYMON, from Barbados aboard the Francis, master Peter Jeffreys, bound for the Leeward Islands on 2 May 1679. [TNA]

WILLIAMS, THOMAS, from Barbados, died in Bristol on 13 November 1773. [GM.43.582]

WILLIAMSON, JOHN, a seaman in Wapping, bound aboard the Tankerfield, master Thomas Burton, for Barbados, probate, 1656, PCC

WILLIAMSON, JOSEPH, a planter in Barbados, died on 13 December 1770. [GM.40.591]

WILLIS, HENRY, from Barbados aboard the Diligence, master Jeremiah Jackson, bound for Boston on 11 February 1679. [TNA]

WILLOUGHBY, MARY ANN, born 1800, daughter of John Willoughby in High Street, wife of Thomas Hall the Inspector General of Hospitals, died 13 March 1859. [St Michael's MI]

WILLOUGHBY, OLIVER, from Barbados aboard the sloop <u>Africa,</u> master Anthony Burgess, bound for Antigua on 8 October 1679. [TNA]

WILLOUGHBY, THOMAS, from Southwark, died in Barbados, Admin., 1649, PCC

WILLOUGHBY, TURPIN, born 1680, died on 2 March 1741. [St Andrew's gravestone]

WILLS, JOHN, from Barbados aboard the <u>Endeavour,</u> master Abraham Newman, bound for Virginia on 17 February 1679. [TNA]

WILSE, FRANCIS, from Barbados aboard the <u>Hope,</u> master Joseph Ball, bound for London on 19 April 1679. [TNA]

WILSON, FLEETWOOD, born 1817, a former Captain of the 8th Hussars, later Auditor General of Barbados, died there on13 September 1862. [GM.ns.2/13.788]

WILSON, JOHN, a merchant from London, from Portsmouth aboard the <u>Gibbons,</u> bound for Barbados in January 1776. [TNA.T47.9/11]

WILSON, RICHARD, a vagrant, suspected thief in Bridewell, bound for Barbados in 1633. [Bridewell Court Minutes]

WILSON, WILLIAM, a planter in Barbados, probate, 1649. [PCC]

WILLSON, WILLIAM, from Barbados aboard the barque <u>Rebecca,</u> master Thomas Williams, bound for Virginia on 15 July 1679. [TNA]

WINDSOR, ..., son of G. H. Windsor, was born in November 1825. [The Barbadian iii]

WINGOTT, JOHN, from Barbados aboard the ketch <u>Prosperous,</u> master David Fogg, bound for Virginia on 8 May 1679. [TNA]

WINNENALL, HUMPHREY, sometime in Barbados, late in Bristol, probate, 1654, PCC

WITHERS, MARY, born1692, wife of Thomas Withers a merchant, died 15 February 1735. [St Michael's MI]

WITHY, Miss, arrived in Bridgetown aboard the Concord from Bristol in February 1825. [The Barbadian iii]

WOLFE, EMANUEL, from Barbados aboard the Thomas and Susan, master David Edwards, bound for Boston on 18 June 1679. [TNA]

WOLFINDEN, JEREMIAH, from Barbados aboard the sloop True Friendship, master Charles Callahan, bound for Nevis on 18 August 1679. [TNA]

WOLVERTON, Captain CHARLES, Governor of Barbados in 1629. [CSPC]

WOOD, Reverend EDWARD DIX, born 1825, second son of Lieutenant General Wood the Commander in Chief of the Windward and Leeward Islands, from Burton, Dorset, died in Queen's House, Barbados, on 31 October 1852. [GM.ns.39.214]

WOOD, EMILY FRANCES, third daughter of Lieutenant General Wood the Commander in Chief of the Windward and Leeward Islands, married Alfred Bury of the 69th Regiment, third son of the Earl of Charleville, in Barbados on 20 June 1854. [GM.ns.42.384]

WOOD, FRANCIS, President of the Ancient Samaritan Charitable Society, in September 1825. [The Barbadian iii]

WOOD, MARY ELIZABETH, fourth daughter of Lieutenant General Wood, Commandant of the Windward and Leeward Islands, married William Shepherd Milner, a Captain of the 69th Regiment, second son of Captain Milner of the Royal Navy, in Barbados on 31 July 1855. [GM.ns.54.531]

WOODBRIDGE, ANN, born 1703, wife of Reverend Dudley Woodbridge, died 3 October 1739. [St James, Hole Town, gravestone]

WOOLFORD, EMILY, daughter of H. Woolford jr., married Captain William Moffatt of the mail boat service on 29 April 1824. [The Barbadian.ii]

WOOLFORD, HENRY, died on 25 November 1825. [The Barbadian iii]

WORKMAN, THOMAS, Casual Receiver in Barbados, from 1759 to 1767. [NRS.GD46.17.1]

WORRELL, Dr JONATHAN, born 1697, died 21 September 1753. Sturges Plantation, St Thomas]

WORRELL, REBECCA, born 1776, widow of Jonathan Worrell, from Barbados, died in East Grinstead on 23 April 1851. [GM.ns.35.685]

WORKMAN, THOMAS, of Barbados, married Mrs Cholmley, widow of Robert Cholmley, in Barbados in 1757. [GM.27.530]

WORSAM, RICHARD, a Councillor of Barbados, died in Philadelphia on 10 May 1766. [GM.36.342]

WORSLEY, HENRY, a former Envoy to Portugal, Governor of Barbados, died on 15 March 1740. [GM.9.148]

WRIGHT, MARY, wife of Lieutenant Colonel Wright of the Royal Engineers, died in Barbados on 6 November 1852. [GM.ns.39.216]

WRIGHT, RICHARD, from Barbados aboard the ketch Mary and Sarah, master George Conway, bound for Carolina on 27 March 1679. [TNA]

WRIGHT, ROBERT, and MARY, from Barbados aboard the ketch Beginning, master William Play, bound for New York on 2 May 1679. [TNA]

YATES, THOMAS, from Barbados aboard the ketch Prospectus, master David Fogg, bound for Virginia on 2 May 1679. [TNA]

YEARWOOD, MARGARET, born 1741, died on 8 September 1825. [The Barbadian iii]

YEARWOOD, THOMAS, from Barbados aboard the barque Endeavour, master Thomas Shaw, bound for Carolina on 4 November 1679. [TNA]

YEATS, THOMAS, died 2 March 1681, husband of Mary Yeats who died 25 August 1682. [St Michael's MI]

YEO, ABRAHAM, a merchant from Bristol, resident in Barbados, probate, 1656, PCC

YOUNG BTYAN T., petitioned for the estate of Enoch Forte Nurse, in June 1825. [The Barbadian iii]

YOUNG, MATHEW, from Barbados aboard the pink Rebecca, master Thomas Williams, bound for Virginia on 18 July 1679. [TNA]

YOUNG, NATHAN, born 1700, a physician, died 1754, father of Nathan Lewis Young, born 1734, a physician, died 28 February 1771, his wife Mary Young, born 1725, died 10 March 1809, their son Lewis Young, born 1765, a physician, died 5 April 1817, his wife Elizabeth Young, born 1774, died 25 February 1816. [St Philip's MI]

SHIPS

Alfred, master William Coulton, at Madeira in July 1807, with one hundred and seventy one passengers, bound for Barbados. [ARM]

Betsey, a brig, master James Hattrick, with three passengers, from Falmouth via Madeira in August 1806 bound for Barbados, also in 1808. [ARM]

Hercules, master Callow Gould, with one passenger, at Madeira bound for Barbados in 1807. [ARM]

Hopewell, a galley, master Thomas Walton Sutton, with twenty passengers, from Falmouth via Madeira bound for Barbados in 1808. [ARM]

Mary of Belfast, trading between Belfast and Barbados in 1726. [NRS.AC9.967]

Sir Sidney Smith, a galley, master James Jeffrey, with one passenger, from Falmouth via Madeira bound for Barbados in 1808. [ARM]

SHIPPING TYPES

Barque – a large decked sea-going merchant vessel

Brig or Brigatine – a two masted, square rigged, sea going vessel

Frigate – a fast, two decked warship

Galley – a low, single-decked vessel, using both sails and oars

Ketch – a small two-masted coastal vessel

Pink – a narrow decked, round sterned bulk carrier

Ship - a three masted, all square sail vessel

Sloop – a single masted vessel

Snow – a brig where the rear mast had a separate upright for the mizzen sail

REFERENCES

ARM   Regional Archives of Madeira

BDA   Barbados Department of Archives

BM   British Museum

BRO   Bristol Record Office

CLRO City of London Record Office

GM   Gentleman's Magazine

HOL   Hotten's Original Lists, J. C. Hotten

LRO   Liverpool Record Office

MI   Monumental Inscription

NRS   National Records of Scotland

PCC   Prerogative Court of Canterbury

PCCol Acts of the Privy Council, Colonial

TNA   The National Archives, Kew

143

www.ingramcontent.com/pod-product-compliance
Lightning Source LLC
Chambersburg PA
CBHW061746270326
41928CB00011B/2398